A NEW HISTORY OF SWANLAND

MEDIEVAL TO STUART TIMES

AND

THE CHURCHES

Swanland Village History Group 2006

ISBN 0-9543440-2-2

Published by Swanland Village History Group
Binding by Colin Burnham 01482 509860

ACKNOWLEDGEMENTS

Our thanks are due to the many individuals whose works are listed in this document and in particular to Geoffrey Collier for the transcription of Lay Subsidy and Manor Court Rolls and sundry wills and other documents from their original medieval Latin, the Rev. Richard Hill for information regarding St. Barnabas Church and Mrs Dyson for access to her memoirs.

Thanks are also expressed to the following people and organizations for the opportunity to access materials in their care:

Beverley Reference Library
Borthwick Institute, University of York
Christ Church, Swanland
The East Riding of Yorkshire Archives
Hatfield History Society
Hull City Archives
Hull Local Studies Library
North Mimms History Society
Paul Leaver, Hull Archives
Penelope Fussel, Archivist of the Drapers' Company
Richard Mortimer, Keeper of the Muniments, Westminster Abbey
The Public Record Office, London
The University of Hull Archives
The West Yorkshire Archive Service, Leeds
Westminster Abbey Archives

Acknowledgements are due to the West Yorkshire Archive Service for permission to reproduce the Manor Court Roll on the cover of the book.

PREFACE

The following book is the third and final volume of a trilogy that covers the history of the village from medieval times to the end of the twentieth century. The present volume deals with the medieval to Stuart periods and with the village churches.

The earlier volumes have been written by one or two individuals from the Swanland Village History Group but the present document includes articles by all of its members. There is also a substantial contribution from Geoffrey Collier.

Early village characters in Swanland have proved to be of real interest. From the 13th and 14th centuries we have the "Lady of Swanland" who "broke by night the walls and dykes made for the preservation of the King's manor at Miton" and from the 15th century, Sir Gerard de Usflet, who is said to have fought at the battle of Agincourt with nine lancers and thirty archers. The village is also fortunate in having an early Independent Chapel (later the Congregational Church) which flourished from 1693. Predating this there are the hidden remains of a Catholic Chapel and Chantry and, following it, an early Primitive Methodist Church and the twentieth century Anglican Church.

Sources for the book have been extensive, with documents coming from all the organizations listed in the acknowledgements above. Discussion has taken place with the various churches. Photographs have been included from the collection initiated at the time of the village's millennium celebrations.

Contributors to the present volume are Derek Brooks, Geoffrey and Linda Collier, Shirley Dalby, Yvonne Dumsday, John Holmes and Glenys Thompson.

Sadly, since reaching the final stages of producing this volume, John Holmes has died. Members of the group are indebted to him for editing all three volumes and for maintaining the momentum in preparing the books.

Contents

LIST OF ILLUSTRATIONS

PREAMBLE

We start this account of early life in Swanland by describing some of the local events which occurred before medieval times.

During the Ice Age, glaciers had pushed down from Scandinavia, Scotland and north-west England carrying with them sand, gravel, clay and boulder that formed the Holderness Plain. It is claimed that the granite boulder outside Boulder Cottage was brought down on ice from Westmorland at least 300,000 years ago. About 10,000 years ago, when ice to the west of the Wolds melted, the River Humber was formed.

The time at which humans first appeared in Swanland is not clear but, from evidence discovered in neighbouring areas, there were inhabitants in this part of England during the Stone Age. Axe heads have been found at Kirkella and North Cave. In the following Bronze Age the famous "Ferriby Boats" were built, dating from about 1650BC or perhaps earlier.

In the second century AD, the geographer Ptolemy wrote about a tribe called the Parisi, who lived in this area five hundred years earlier. They left the remains of their burial sites beneath small mounds (barrows) surrounded by square ditches. Examples appear at Market Weighton, Burton Fleming and other places. A square barrow has recently been discovered at Melton during excavations prior to road works. On the same site a Bronze Age Barrow and a Romano-British corn drier have been discovered.

The Romans invaded Britain in AD43 but advanced no further than the southern bank of the Humber until AD71, when the ninth legion crossed the river into the lands of the Parisi. In the second half of the fourth century a series of signal stations was built on the east coast. The Roman centre for local government was Petuaria (Brough) and aerial photographs have disclosed a Roman road from Welton leading diagonally across Melton Bottoms, so Roman soldiers may well have passed through the site of modern day Swanland to help man these outposts. The soldiers were recalled by 410AD to defend Rome and none were left in Britain.

The site of Red Cliff, to the west of North Ferriby, dates from the middle of the first century AD and has been described as a "port of trade" serving the Parisi and the Romans at old Winteringham on the south bank. A number of Staters, Britain's earliest coins from the first century A.D. have been discovered in this area at Ferriby.

1

Between the fifth and eighth centuries there is evidence of Anglo Saxon occupation both to the west and to the north of Swanland. The area of Anglo Saxon England in which the site of Swanland was situated was called Deira and was part of Northumbria. This ran from the Rivers Ribble and Humber to the border with Scotland. Silver coins known as Sceats, in use during this period, have been found at Welton and in Beverley. Those found at Beverley were dated 737-758AD.

793 AD saw the first invasion of these isles by the Vikings and by 880 AD most of Northumbria and East Anglia were ruled by the Danes. In the treaty of 886, when this part of the country was subject to Danelaw, Swanland was part of the Norse Kingdom of York.

We now turn to the Vikings and to Swanland's name.

THE VIKINGS AND SWANLAND'S NAME

'Tis the hard grey weather
Breeds hard English men.

Come; and strong within us
Stir the Vikings blood;
Bracing brain and sinew
Blow, thou wind of God!

There has been a traditional belief in Swanland that the village name was associated with that of the Danish King Swein, and that it derived from "Swein's land". In 1943, however, a much respected Hull historian, Tom Sheppard, suggested that this was mistaken. He took the name simply to mean " the land of the Swan"[1] and found support from John Nicholson[2] who, in 1926, had examined the various historical spellings of the name and concluded that the second syllable came from the Danish word lund or grove so that the name meant "swans' grove". A further conclusion was arrived at in 1937 by A.H.Smith who thought it was derived from "Svan's wood".[3]

It is interesting to look at the background to these propositions. A brief list of the various historical spellings of the name is given at the end of this article.

Swein's Land -The Danish Connection

The belief that Swanland's name derived from one of the Danish Kings, Swein, appears to come from Thomas Thompson F.S.A. who, writing in 1870, stated:

> " Sweine, like the Saxon Ella, found the necessity of selecting some high land on the shores of the Humber from which he might decry any hostile fleet coming to attack him…………..Such a position he found in Swanland, so called after him (Sweine's land), when he took up his quarters there…"[4]

Thompson writes with great confidence and supports his assertions by claiming to find marks of ancient Danish camps in old enclosures on the open fields called "Ferriby Mounts". Unfortunately, whilst clearly familiar with the Norse sagas, he gives no reference to particular sources.

The present study has sought to obtain corroboration of this derivation. There is certainly evidence that the Danes were present in the area. This is provided by the Anglo Saxon Chronicle and by the place names of nearby villages.

We read in the Anglo Saxon Chronicle for the year 1069 that:

> "...three sons of king Swein with 240 ships came from Denmark into the Humber, ...There they were met by Prince Edgar .... with the Northumbrians, and all the people in the country. Forming an immense host, riding and marching in high spirits, they all resolutely advanced on York and stormed and destroyed the castle, ...slaying many hundreds of Frenchmen and carrying off great numbers to their ships.....The troops lay all winter in the Humber where the king could not reach them."[5]

Swein's Fleet, Thompson says, lay up the Ouse, at a place on which it has conferred the name of Swinefleet.

Again, in 1070:

> "king Swein came into the Humber from Denmark and the people of the country met him and came to terms with him, thinking that he was to conquer the whole country."[6]

An earlier king, Swein Forkbeard, the father of King Canute, had also sailed into the Humber, establishing a camp at Gainsborough, where he died in 1014.[7] There is reference to the ferry at North Ferriby being: "safeguarded at the command of King Canute in about 1025."[8] It is clear, however, that the Swein that Thompson refers to is the later of the two, since he refers to the march to York and mentions the date as 1069.

A description of Swein Forkbeard's ships[9], with their: "gaudy paint, gilt figureheads and rows of shields around the gunnels", paints a colourful picture of the Viking presence.

Place names provide further evidence of the Danes. Those close to Swanland include Anlaby, Tranby, Ferriby, Willerby and Wauldby. The ending "by" denotes a village or settlement. Further, as mentioned earlier, it is claimed that the "..land" in Swanland derived from the Scandinavian lund, meaning a wood or grove.

The Land of the Swans

Sheppard's suggestion that the name simply means "the land of the swan" was essentially based on his belief that, historically, swans were common in the neighbourhood.[10] Swanland had two meres on which they could settle. His view was supported by Nicholson's analysis of the place name. Amongst other references, Sheppard cites the presence of swans at the earl of Northumberland's castles at Leconfield and Wressle (1512) a swan token in the museum in Hull (1666) and the existence of a Swanners Court for the King at Hempholme (1708). Perhaps more persuasive is the fact that a black swan surmounted the second Haldenby coat of arms.[11] The Haldenbys were Lords of the Manor of Swanland.

Swein or Swannery

Where then does this leave us? Does Swanland's name derive from King Swein or was it simply a land of swans?

The fact that Sheppard demonstrates that there were swans in the area does not prove that they gave it its name, although the presence of a swan on the Haldenby coat of arms is suggestive.

Equally the present attempt to find corroborative evidence for the name deriving from Swein's land has proved unsuccessful. J.G.Patton's attempt to find corroboration in 1943 also failed. All we can prove at present is that Swein was present in the Humber area. Swanland was very small at that time. It was not mentioned in the Domesday Book but it is of course possible, and even likely, that Swein could have used the high ground around the village to establish lookout posts.

Regrettably that is where we must leave it for the present. Perhaps the future holds evidence that is lacking at the moment and the matter will then be resolved. For the time being it seems to the writer that it is a possibility, but no more, that Swanland's name derives from a Viking King and "can stir our Viking blood".

Historical Spellings of the Name of Swanland

Suenland	*Pipe Rolls*	*1189*
Swanneslond	*Chronica de Melsa*	*1210*
Swaneslund	*Close Rolls etc.*	*1237-1305*
Swanelonde	*Westminster Abbey Muniments*	*1282*
Swanneslund	*Westminster Abbey Muniments*	*1288*
Swanneslund	*Charter Rolls etc.*	*1293-1342*
Swanysland	*Yorkshire Inquisitions*	*1301*
Swanlund	*Yorkshire Inquisitions etc*	*1303-1559*
Swannelund	*Registers of the Archbishops of York*	*1304*
Swanlond	*Westminster Abbey Muniments*	*1309*
Swanlond	*Westminster Abbey Muniments*	*1315*
Swanlound	*Westminster Abbey Muniments*	*1316*
Swaunlund	*Westminster Abbey Muniments*	*1317*
Swaunnelunde	*Westminster Abbey Muniments*	*1322*
Swanlunde	*Westminster Abbey Muniments*	*1322*
Swannelond	*Westminster Abbey Muniments*	*1324*
Swaneslaunde	*Westminster Abbey Muniments*	*1324*
Swaneslonde	*Westminster Abbey Muniments*	*1366*

THE MEDIEVAL PERIOD

TIMELINE

Swanland		The Nation	
		William the Conqueror crowned King of England	1066
1069	King Swein sails into the River Humber		
		The Domesday Book assembled	1086
1140	The Priory of North Ferriby is founded		
		Murder of Thomas à Beckett at Canterbury	1179
1189	First mention of the name Swanland		
1210	Record of Swanland's association with the de Vescy family	King John signs the Magna Carta	1215
By 1286	Loretta de Furnival (the Lady of Swanland), is married to John de Usflet	Roger Bacon (1214-1293) discovers Gunpowder	
		By statute of Edward I, all males over seven had to be trained in archery	1272-1307
1316	Loretta with others broke the walls and dykes of the King's Manor at Myton		
1332	Earliest surviving tax records The Lay Subsidy Roll		
		Two thirds of Yorkshire's population wiped out by the Black Death	1349
1337	Population of Hull estimated to be 1557		
1381	Poll Tax returns available for the lost village of Haldenby	The Peasants' Revolt against the Poll Tax	1381

THE DOMESDAY BOOK

In 1085, at his Christmas Court, William the Conqueror had:

> " much thought…about this country and .. sent his men into every shire and had them find out how many (units of land) there were…and what or how much everyone in England had."[12]

This was the basis of the Domesday Book, so called after the Day of Judgement, against which there could be no appeal. It was to be used for taxation purposes, for liability for military service and as a record of land holdings.

Swanland was not specifically mentioned in the survey but may have been part of the manor of Ferebi (North Ferriby) or of Aluengi (which included Kirkella). This would not be surprising as there are other examples of parcels of land omitted, which were parts of larger manors. Wyke (subsequently to become Kingston-upon-Hull) was such a parcel in the Manor of Myton.

A note in a work relating to early Yorkshire Charters, mentioning North Ferriby[13], reads:

> "Ralph de Mortemer had the manor there…(and) within the manor were included the township of Swanland and the place called Braithwaite, now lost."

Certainly by 1210, after Eustace de Vescy had succeeded de Mortemer to the Lordship of North Ferriby, there is reference to: "..his (de Vescy's) men of Swanneslond"[14] and by 1316 Laura de Usflet held "Swanland cum Ferriby" jointly with the Prior of Ferriby.

On the other hand there is a view put forward by Wilson-Barkworth, a member of the East Riding Antiquarian Society in the 1920s, which suggests that Swanland was included in the 1200 acres of land held by Ralph de Mortemer in the district of Alvengi.[15]

The present writer is inclined to believe that Swanland was part of the manor of Ferebi, for which the entry in the Domesday Book reads:

> "Manor. In Ferebi, Eddiua had ten carucates of land for geld. The land is to five ploughs. Ralph has there now fourteen villanes with three ploughs. A priest (is) there, and a church. T.R.E., it was worth one hundred shillings; now, sixty shillings."[16]

A carucate, amounted to about 120 acres, but depended on the quality of the soil

From this we deduce that de Mortemer's estate in North Ferriby comprised about 1200 acres and that he had 14 villagers attached to it. The 1200 acres was sufficient to employ five plough teams. Mortemer had three ploughs there. (A full plough team was eight oxen). The villagers, called villanes (or villeins) were in bondage to their Lord, owing him rent and services, including the ploughing and reaping of his land for a number of days each year. In return they were allotted about 15 acres (a bovate) for their own use. They were annexed to the Lord's person and could not marry without his permission. At the time of Edward the Confessor, the land had returned 100 shillings, but in 1085 it was worth only 60 shillings. Gent attributes the reduction in value to the invasion of King Swein in 1069, and writes:

> "...Swein, King of Denmark, ..coming into the Humber; and with his soldiers having destroyed all that was least valuable in the country on both sides of the river,
> ...proceeded to York, and miserably ruin'd the circumadjacent parts for several miles,
> ...Among those near Hull that suffered such lamentable destruction an ancient manuscript has particularly recorded the villages of Ferriby, Drypool, Sculcoates and Myton"[17]

Swein's invasion was revenged by William's "Harrying of the North".

The Ralph de Mortimer mentioned in the Domesday Book entry held land spread over twelve counties. It was divided in this way to prevent power being concentrated in any individual's hand. He derived his name from Mortimer-en-Lions, between Neufchatel and Armale. His chief estate was at Wigmore Castle in Herefordshire. Eddiue, from whom he received his lands in Yorkshire and Lincolnshire, is thought to have been Edith, queen consort to King Harold. [18]

The berewicks, (detached estates), of Wauldby, Riplingham, Totfled, Myton, Wolfreton and Hessle belonged to the manor of North Ferriby.

POPULATION

In his *History of Hull*, Gent writes:

> "This country (the East Riding) was but thinly inhabited before the Norman Conquest: That as the Danes had, from Time to Time, destroyed most part of it; so, it lay waste and untilled, in many Places, even to the Time of this Survey, (The Domesday Book).
>
> ....That Ferriby, tho' it contained not above thirty Houses, was then the chiefest Town of this part of the country; those lesser scarcely exceeding Twelve each..."[17] If he is correct then, in 1085, Swanland comprised not more than twelve houses.

The Pipe Rolls of 1187 are consistent with Swanland and North Ferriby remaining small communities.[19] Together the villages owed only 33s to the King, whilst by comparison Driffield owed £12 19s 8d and Pocklington £7 6s 8d.

By 1332 the Lay Subsidy (tax) returns[20] mention twenty-one households. (The number could have been greater as the poorest of the villagers were exempt this tax). By 1672 Hearth Tax returns[21] indicate the village to be home to 35 households. From all of this it may be concluded that during the period under consideration Swanland was but a very small settlement.

It may be of general interest to know the population of the country as a whole and of some of the local towns at this time. These were as follows:

1085	England	1.25 to 2.15 million
Late 13th.C	England	5 to 7 million
Mid 15th.C	England	2.25 million*
1377	York	7,248
	Lincoln	3,412
	Beverley	2,663
	Hull	1,557

The decline resulted from the Plague.

THE MEDIEVAL VILLAGE

The Manorial System

From the eleventh century, a manorial system of landholding developed in England that survived in certain forms until the early twentieth century.

John Norden, writing in 1607, described the manor as "a little common wealth, whereof the Tenants are the members, the Lande the bulke and the Lord (of the Manor) the head".[22]

Certainly, the system was a hierarchical one, having its origins in the feudal arrangement whereby land was held on condition of homage and service to a superior lord. At the top of the tree was the king, who granted to members of the nobility the rights to specified lands in return for their military service in times of conflict. Such persons, who held their lands directly from the crown, were known as tenants in chief and, in the case of large holdings, might allocate certain manors to subordinate lords.

Within a given manor, the lord retained the best land for his personal use and support, and this was known as the demesne land. The manor house and its immediate environs were known as the capital messuage but the total size of the manor could vary from a hundred acres or so to many thousands of acres. Nor was it necessarily centred around one community but might be spread over a number of townships or vills. From a local viewpoint, it is interesting to note that the manor of Swanland had grazing rights in the pastures of Myton.

Any land not required by the lord for his personal use, or for pasture, was tenanted but there were two distinct types of tenancy: free and unfree.

Freemen paid a fixed money rent and sometimes contributed light labour. However, they were free to dispose of their land as they wished, without reference to the manorial courts. The unfree tenants, also known as villeins or bondsmen, were obliged to pay for their lands by labouring on the lord's demesne for a specified number of days each year. In addition they might be obliged to pay a money rent or a rent in the form of produce. They were also subject to significant restrictions on their personal freedom, being required, for example, to seek the permission of the lord if they wished to educate their sons or if one of their children wished to marry. In the latter case a payment known as a merchet was required, though in some manors it was only enforced if the marriage was to a person outside the manor.[23]

Sometimes an individual might occupy lands by both types of tenure, with certain holdings as a freeman and others as a villein.

At the lowest level of the manorial hierarchy were the cottars, otherwise known as borders or tenants-at-will. These persons were directly employed, either by the lord or by large freeholders, and rewarded with living accommodation in the form of a cottage and a bit of garden.

In the middle of the fourteenth century a catastrophic reduction in the population occurred as a consequence of the Black Death and plague remained endemic in Britain for a further three hundred years. Manorial records indicate that, in some cases, up to two thirds of the tenants may have died at the height of the epidemic. Faced with great difficulties in finding new tenants to cultivate the land, the lords had to offer more advantageous terms to the villeins, with greater personal liberty, and the requirement to provide labour services on the demesne was gradually replaced by money payment. In time, villeins became known as customary holders, being deemed to hold their land 'according to the custom of the manor'.[24]

By the sixteenth century, the tenure of customary holders had been further strengthened. They also became known as copyholders, their holdings being recorded in the rolls of the manor court, of which they were given a copy of the relevant entry to confirm their entitlement. Copyhold was only finally abolished in 1922.

It was sometimes possible for customary holders to take on additional land by way of lease, though this option was not available in all manors. Similarly, tenants generally had the right to sub-let their land.[25]

The type of holding greatly influenced the security of family inheritance. When a tenant died a payment in kind, known as a heriot, was immediately due to the lord of the manor. This usually took the form of the best living beast on the holding. In the case of a freehold, the inheritor of the holding also had to make a money payment to the lord, known as a relief, and often equal to a year's rent, upon entering into the tenancy.

Rather different arrangements applied to customary holders, of which there were two categories. Customary holders for life enjoyed only limited security, their tenancy being restricted either to the duration of their own lives, or sometimes to their own, their spouses' and their eldest sons' lives. On the death of a tenant for life, the lord was free to make a new tenancy with whomever he should choose.

Customary holders of inheritance could pass their lands on to an heir in accordance with the customs of the manor. In many cases, but not all, the heir would be the eldest son. As with freeholders, a heriot would be payable on the death of an existing tenant, and the new customary holder would be required to pay a fine to the lord on entering into the tenancy. Depending on the custom of the manor, such a fine could be fixed or arbitrary. In the latter case, the lord was entitled to set the fine at the highest level that was likely to be affordable and this clearly disadvantaged poorer tenants. Over time, entry fines generally settled to a level equivalent to one or two years' rent.[26]

All these arrangements required appropriate administrative systems. A lord who held a number of manors would usually appoint a steward to manage his estates. Each manor would have a bailiff responsible for matters of day-to-day running and, below him, a foreman or reeve to oversee the cultivation of the land and the sale of stock. A reeve was usually a tenant, undertaking this duty on a rotating yearly basis, and might be excused the payment of rent while holding this office.

Other officials might also be appointed, such as the hayward to oversee haymaking, harvesting and the maintenance of hedges; the pinder responsible for rounding up stray animals and confining them in the pinfold; and even the ale-taster, responsible for ensuring that ale was of an acceptable quality and dispensed in proper measures. At a time when the quality of drinking water was both variable and dubious, the functions of the latter were of added importance and he would also collect fees for ale made under licence.

It is thus apparent that the manor was a social concept as much as a territorial one and crucial to the regulation of that society were the manor courts, of which there were two types.

The court baron was the court established to enforce the rules set down as 'the custom of the manor' and to deal with offences against them. Its name is derived from the original granting of manors to the barons by the king, with the accompanying right to hold a court for their proper administration. Sittings of the court would normally be presided over by the steward or the bailiff on behalf of the lord, supported by a jury drawn from the tenants, usually twelve in number. It was in this court that new customary tenants took possession of their land through the procedure of surrender and admission which was duly recorded in the court records. Other business would include the imposition of fines for minor civil offences, such as failure to observe or maintain the boundaries of a holding or damage caused by stray animals.

The other type of manor court was known as the court leet that met twice a year, normally at Easter or Michaelmas. It could deal with minor criminal offences and might also appoint the constable (another rotating office) who was responsible for imposing law and order. From the sixteenth century its functions were increasingly superceded by those of the Justices of the Peace and the Quarter Sessions, and it progressively declined in importance.

In practice, the distinct jurisdictions of the court leet and the court baron were not always clearly separated. The same jurymen would often serve for both. The proceedings of the court leet were usually simply noted in the records of the court baron but in any case the surviving manorial court records are now a rich source of information on life in rural England. During the medieval period, these records were written on rolls of parchment but from Tudor times onwards, they were bound into books.[23]

Other manorial records include various types of survey, instigated by the lord, listing the different kinds of revenue to be had from rents and dues and other sources.

Court Rolls of the Manor of Swanland

The only known surviving records of the Swanland manor courts are nowadays in the care of the West Riding Archive Service at Sheepscar, Leeds. They comprise records of some thirty sittings of the court between 1492 and 1579. In other words, they span the period from the reign of the first Tudor monarch to the last and provide a unique insight into the governance of the village at that time. Sadly, records of any earlier (medieval) sittings do not appear to have survived.

Both types of manor court are represented, the court baron and the court leet. On some occasions the record is explicitly stated to be that of the court baron; at other times it is described as a record of 'The court, with a view of frankpledge'. The [re]view of frankpledge is a commonly encountered alternative term for the court leet. In other instances again, the record is simply headed as the proceedings of "The court of .... Stapleton and .... Haldenby", the actual names being those of the particular members of these two families who shared the lordship of the manor at the time. Suffice it to say that, very often, both aspects of the business of manor courts are covered at the same sitting.

Up to the time of the present study, no known translation of these documents into modern English (from the abbreviated legal Latin) has been available. A full English transcript of the court rolls for 1511[28] is now given in Appendix 1.

At that time the Lordship of Swanland was held jointly by Brian Stapleton and Robert Haldenby and this is an account of their court for that year. The two sittings of the court reported here were held on Tuesday 20 April and Wednesday 7 October 1511. They were presided over by the steward, Robert Constable, whose status is

15

given as that of a knight. The steward was often a person of some legal knowledge, at least at the level of manor courts and often beyond, because he could be required to represent the lord(s) in other jurisdictions. The business transacted here reflects the functions both of the court baron and of the court leet.

The jurors are first listed by name, in the groups of two or three in which they would take the oath.

The first business of the first sitting concerns a matter of landholding. It appears that the heir to the lands of the deceased Walter Rudston had been extremely tardy in fulfilling his duty to attend the court to do homage and to pay a 'fine' on entering to his holding. The local bailiff (not named) was therefore ordered to distrain the lands until the defaulting heir should make an appearance.

There then follow the various 'presentments' of the decisions of the jury regarding alleged breaches of the custom of the manor, or of the peace. These typically result in the imposition of monetary penalties (amercements or *misericordia*). Persons found to be culpable are said to be *in misericordiam* – literally, 'in the mercy' or (as we should now say) 'at the mercy' of the lord (of the manor).

The first of these illustrates the severity with which the court regarded theft. A local woman had been accused of the theft of a small quantity of barley (perhaps about a cupful) and the household from which she allegedly took it might well have been that of an employer. She was fined a shilling which, for a woman in lowly circumstances, seems a great deal compared to penalties imposed for other misdemeanours.

One of the frequent offenders against the custom of the manor was the Prior of Ferriby, a person of considerable standing in his own right and possessed of substantial livestock. He frequently exceeded his grazing rights and appears to have treated the Swanland court with blatant contempt. Moreover he, and others, repeatedly failed to attend sittings of court when required as a condition of their land holdings in Swanland. It might be inferred that the Swanland court was conducted in a rather casual manner at this time and that may be a reason why relatively few records have survived from the early sixteenth century and earlier.

Sittings of the manor court were also the occasion for stating or reaffirming the custom of the manor in terms of regulations, or *pains* as they were widely known, and we have several examples of that here. No one must allow his or her animals to stray into the arable fields, under penalty of a fine. Everyone must take their turns in bringing stones for the repair of the common road: the tenants to cart six loads apiece during the spring, the cottagers to gather (or presumably dig) the same. Unlawful grazing in the pastures of Ferriby was also punishable, though elderly widows appear to have been treated more leniently in this regard (after all, it was only Ferriby!) Finally, retribution would surely follow if any person presumed to cut or move crops belonging to the lord and, from now on, gleaning on the demesne was to be banned.

The record of the second sitting follows a similar pattern to the first, the final entry dealing with two men who had been involved in a fight. This is clearly the province of the court leet. They were each fined ten shillings (3s 4d for making an affray and 6s 8d for drawing blood). It may well be that weapons were involved but, in any case, these were heavy penalties.

These reports of a particular year's court transactions are broadly typical of the surviving records as a whole. The quality of the reports, and indeed of the handwriting, varies over time, some accounts being fairly cursory, others much more formal and detailed. For example, in the records for 1579,[29] a question of landholding involves a review of the matter back to the pre-dissolution tenure by the Prior of Ferriby.

It also appears that, in the latter part of the sixteenth century, the lords administered the manor much more rigorously. Up to fifty fines might be imposed in one court sitting. Furthermore the names of all tenants, both free and unfree, were recorded on the roll and any not attending at court in person were required to pay an *essoin*, normally a few pence delivered by proxy.[30] On the court roll, the annotation *ess.* appears above the name of any person thus excused. Unauthorised absentees would be fined as usual.

Occupations

In medieval times, small rural communities like Swanland had to be self-sufficient. Though most people would be directly engaged in the cultivation of the fields or in animal husbandry, many would also acquire some basic related skills in, for example, joinery, weaving or butchery. Where the size of the community warranted it, some individuals would specialise and devote their full time to these occupations, developing these trades in their own right.

Additionally, or alternatively, some members of the community would undertake duties that were necessary for the operation of the manorial system.

As the practice of using surnames developed the specialist trades and the manorial functions came into use as secondary names and eventually family names, most of which are still in use in modern times. Reeve, Hayward and Pinder all trace their origins back to the manorial tasks undertaken by those to whom these names were first attributed. Similarly, the name of Constable derives from the manorial or parochial office of those first entrusted with enforcement of the criminal law within a township.

With regard to specialised occupations, the range of associated surnames is vast and varied. For example, whereas names such as Carpenter were widely encountered, other specialist skills within the woodworking trades were developed over time and names such as Wheelwright, Cartwright and Wainwright all came into use.

Many modern occupational surnames of ancient origin have rather less obvious derivations but are interesting to note here. These include:

Chapman –	a general dealer
Chandler –	a candle maker
Cissor –	a tailor
Cooper –	a cask or barrel maker
Cordwainer -	a shoemaker
Fletcher –	a flesh hewer or butcher
Lepar –	a basket maker
Lorimer –	a maker of spurs and bridles
Mercer –	a draper
Poulter –	a poultryman
Souter –	a shoemaker
Theaker –	a thatcher
Walker –	a fuller (a person who cleansed and thickened woollen cloth by immersing it in water and treading or walking on it)

Monetary Values

A study of medieval records yields interesting information on the value of money in those times and on the relative worth of goods and of labour. The relative values of produce and other goods were often significantly different from those of today.

The basic units of money were, of course, those of pounds (£), shillings (s) and pence (d), with a pound being worth twenty shillings or two hundred and forty pence. Other units were also in common use however, including the groat (a third of a shilling, or 4d) and the mark (two thirds of a pound, or 13s 4d). Useful indications of the value of goods and commodities can be gleaned from the fourteenth century records of the Poll Tax and the Lay Subsidy Rolls.

Approximate values were as follows:

Wheat and barley –	4s 6d per quarter (28 lb or approx. 13 kilo)
Peas –	3s 4d per quarter

Horses	–	5s to 10s each
Cows	–	7s to 10s each
Sheep and pigs	–	1s each
Goats		2s each

On the other hand, an indication of the relative affluence, or ability to pay tax, is given by the rates of tax for which various classes were liable in the Poll Tax of 1377-80, as follows:

	£	s	d
Dukes and archbishops	6	13	4
Earls and countesses	4	0	0
Barons and baronets	2	0	0
Justices	5	0	0
Attorneys		2	8
Mayors	2	0	0
Great merchants	1	0	0
Small merchants and artificers		6	8
Farmers and cattle dealers		6	8
Innkeeper {		3	4
to		1	0

EARLY ROADS AND HOUSES

Roads

Before the establishment of a structured road system, early travellers used the high ground of the Ridgeway Routes or the earthworks of ditches, such as Danes Dike, as tracks. Recent excavations at Melton have revealed ditches two metres deep running parallel to Melton Bottoms. Were these the beginnings of Great Gutter Lane? When the Romans came, a structured plan of road building was established for troop movements.

The oldest known road to pass through the village of Swanland is of Roman origin. It was observed on aerial photographs taken prior to an excavation on Welton Wold.[31] The road proceeds from Welton, diagonally across Melton Bottoms 200 metres east of Mill Hill, and then travels over the fields, crossing Dale Road in the region of its junction with Northfield. If it continued in a straight line, it would make for Wawne ferry. It has not yet been exposed, although a watch was conducted when the Westerdale development was taking place, and a chalk road was noticed running in the field behind Chantry Way,

When the Romans left, many of their metalled roads fell into decay. Few roads were built but rather they evolved as tracks with the need to travel from one place to another.

Swanland village was planned in typical medieval manner with a main street having parallel back roads on both sides. The properties and farms were situated on the main street and ran through to the back roads. The main road became slightly sunken through the years and the footpaths in Main Street to the east of the present grocers' shop, and in West End, can be seen to be considerably higher than the road. The oldest properties in the village, the row of shops opposite Kemp Road, have a high step, because the road in front of them has worn away. Straightening has modified the only back road that still exists, which is Tranby Lane.

The Pre-Enclosure Map of the village shows that land surrounding houses was already enclosed. At the time of the open fields, dating from manorial times, the farm houses were situated on the village main street. Farmers went out to the fields to work and brought their produce back to the farm. The oxen and horses had to be penned somewhere, so the land that the farmers owned in the village, running from the main street to the back roads, was fenced off to contain the animals. During the day, cows and sheep were taken out onto the grass verges and balks to graze under the supervision of a shepherd or cowherd. This practice was still continuing at the end of the nineteenth century, when the newly formed Council was asking to receive payments for grazing the roadsides.

In medieval times, another track belonging to Swanland township ran along the Humber bank. The parishioners of St. Mary's, Lowgate, buried their dead at their mother church at Ferriby and had to pass along it on route. Swanland villagers grumbled about the upkeep of a track used by the inhabitants of Ferriby or Hull.

The original roads of Swanland were constructed of chalk taken from a pit near to the former mill, and from a Manor Court Roll of 1511-12 (the time of the Haldenbys) we learn that:

> "It is pained that each person should make six cartings, before the feast of St. John the Baptist next to come, for the making up of the common way, under penalty of whosoever (shall default)12d. And (those) who stay in the cottages should collect stones, each of them to the making of six cartings, under penalty of whichever carting 4d."
> (See Appendix 1.)

In passing it is interesting to note that a local archaeologist, Mortimer, makes mention of the chalk surfaced roads. He says:

> "Chalk slurry that accumulated on road surfaces was scraped off. The slurry was then spread onto house floors, where after a few days it set hard. It then lasted several years before needing renewing."

Roads surrounding the Village and their Names (See Fig 1)

Woodgates Lane is an ancient thoroughfare that is of interest. The northern end no longer exists but its route across the fields can be followed by five or six chalk pits used for its repair. These can be seen on older Ordnance Survey maps. The route of the Lane is peculiar as it appears not to connect Ferriby to Swanland but to bypass the village. It can be observed that the Lane curves round and links with Eppleworth Road and on to Cottingham, in fact directly to Baynard Castle. If the road were to be extended in the other direction down to the river in Ferriby it would arrive at a small jetty. One can speculate on the reason. Was this road a way to the Stutvilles's fortified Manor at Cottingham? Was it the route for Cave stone to be transported there for its building? It would certainly provide a convenient method for Swanland villagers to go to Cottingham. They could take Crowther Lane, veer left into Tom Potts Lane, turn right into Woodgates Lane and travel on through Raywell and Eppleworth. By turning north at Raywell a similar journey would take one to Braffords or Braithwaite (a detached part of Swanland parish).

Before the Enclosures the road that runs north from the pond was short, no longer than 140 yards in length. It terminated at "The Pinfold" (an enclosure for stray animals). Radiating from "The Pinfold" was a back road to West Field Lane, another back road that curved around and joined Main Street at its easterly end, and a branch of this road leading to Westella. The portion between Beech Hill and Pinfold was named West Ella Road according to the wills of the Shaw family. A further road or track struck off in a north-westerly direction, crossing the now disused part of Woodgates Lane and carrying on to Melton Bottoms where its continuation still exists. The whole of this road was called Tom Potts Lane.

The road joining Ferriby to Swanland is an ancient way that splits into two a little before entering the village. The present writer has always had a fascination with roads and has recently been speculating on the reason for the split. The conclusion has been that it was due to the intended destination of the travellers. West Leys was the shortest route for the monks from Ferriby Priory to get to their Chapel of Ease off Westfield Lane, whilst the other branch (Kemp Road) led to the village and the Priory's farm.

An old track called Gate Gate Trod used to run directly towards Hessle from the corner of Kemp Road and Tranby Lane before the Enclosures. The word Trod has been used to describe a garden path and this may suggest that the track to Hessle was merely a path or bridleway. It certainly crossed the tilled land of the strip fields. The word Gate in the previous two road names could suggest that they were gated roads. This seems unlikely, as land was not then enclosed. The word Gate has other meanings. If you rent land today on Beverley Common (the Westwood or Figham) the charge would be by the gate. A Gate is a measure of land similar to an acre and is the amount of pasture required to feed one cow or three sheep. So Gate Gate Trod would have passed two Gates of land. Gate is also Norse for Road, so that a third possibility is that Gate Gate Trod could mean a path between two roads which is in fact what it was. But why Woodgates? On the Pre-Enclosure Map there is an area close to Riplingham Road named Woodgates flat. This is close to a wood presently known as "Nut Wood". It was once common practice to run pigs in woods where they grubbed for roots and acorns. A woodgate would therefore be land for the free range of pigs.

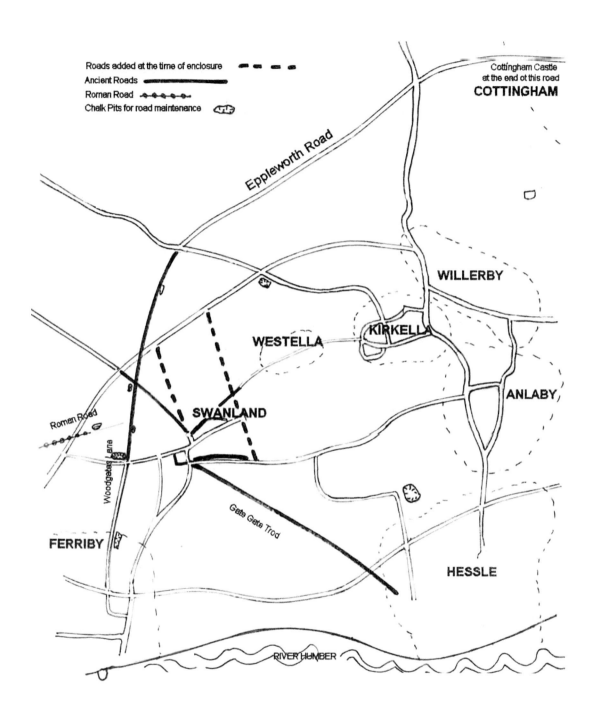

Fig. 1 Map of Swanland with Medieval roads added

Early Houses

Archaeological Excavation

The remains of what are believed to be the earliest houses in Swanland were uncovered in 1989 by Derek Brooks, Patrick Norfolk and others. They were found in a field bounded by Main Street, Beech Hill Road and Beech Hill House. The site is now occupied by the St. Barnabas Drive development.

In the two weeks just prior to the development, a rapid archaeological survey was made of what appeared to be "house platforms" which stood out as undulations. The archaeological survey is described fully in Appendix 2, and shown in outline on Fig. 2. The houses found were of 15th to 16th Century in date. With the possibility that somewhere close at hand there may have been something from the 13th Century.

The house on Site 1 measured aprox. 12 x 4.5m. It is a typical house of a peasant medieval farmer who would live in one half of the house and keep his cow in the other half. The hearth was on the floor, there would be no chimney just a hole in the roof. Wood would be used for the fire although coal was recorded from the site.

Finds from the site included:

Metal	Many nails some of which were of the horse shoe variety Keyhole horse shoes A hinge crook for door or window A Jeton or Nuremburg token inscribed Hans Schultz Nor
Pottery	Mostly 16th C. Humberware possibly from Holme on Spalding Moor. There were also several shards of 12-13th.C Orange ware. This came from the extreme northwest where it was impossible to excavate.
Bone	A large variety of animal bones mostly butchered sheep and cow.
Stone	Chalk Spindle Whorl.
Glass	A piece of very blackened flat glass.
Brick & Tile	Bricks 10x 5x 2in. are found on site, mostly used as hearth tiles. It was noted that the hearth tiles were reused.
Walls	These were built from both chalk and oolitic limestone also squared.

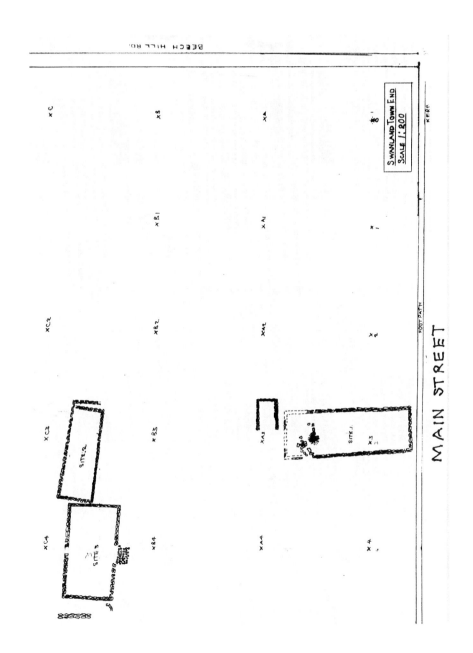

Fig. 2 Site of Archaeological Excavations– East End Main Street

Paved Areas   Outside the south entrance of site 3 there was an area of chalk and cobbles. Although only a small area was uncovered it would appear that the area down the slope to the pond was cobbled. The inside area of site 1 round the hearth had limestone slabs and chalk

14-16A West End

The row of four shops 14 to 16A West End was originally built slightly later than those uncovered in Main Street. A piece of wood sent off for dendrochronology came back with a 15th C date. Before the shops, these buildings were cottages and before that a single farmhouse of timber framed structure. The walls have been replaced with brick; the only part that tells us its origin is two wall plates that run down the edge of the front.

In number 16, where the timber is visible, mortice holes can be seen where the upright and diagonal timbers fitted. This house also has the original inglenook fireplace. The pad stones that supported the uprights can be observed below the east wall.

During the medieval period, farmers lived in the village and went out to work in the fields. Following the Enclosures, farmhouses were built on the farms and accommodation for the workers was needed in the villages. This would account for this farmhouse being converted into four cottages. Fig 3 shows a model made by Derek Brooks of the farmhouse, as it would have been.

Fig. 3 Model of how the farmhouse would have looked when built

26

Ancient Foundations – 40 West End

When Queensbury Way was built in 1958, the writer was asked to examine some masonry that was being exposed in the building trenches. Although this find was reported, there were no requirements at that time to carry out archaeological excavations prior to building. A watching brief was conducted by the writer who noted a wall some 50M long, extending northwards from the corner of the garden of 40 West End. When the writer purchased Number 40 during the house extension a corner of this wall was revealed.

The masonry footings found at 40 West End were quite enormous, the curtain wall was 76cm thick, doubled in thickness by buttresses. Each buttress was 2.28M long and there was only 76cm between them. It is not known what length of wall is buttressed but a return wall running parallel to West End was found when excavating in the entrance of 38 West End showing a similar construction. The wall was built from oolitic limestone that is found naturally at Cave. It sits on two courses of chalk blocks and its core contains medieval brick rubble (brick size 10 x 5 x 2in.). It is bonded with coarse lime mortar. The wall footings in Queensbury Way had bevelled plinth stones incorporated. If this enormous structure were standing today it would no doubt be described as Swanland Castle. The finds on the site are quite sparse. There are some sandstone window mullions, a bone knife handle and shards of pottery. The latter are dated to the 16th century.

Patton, in his book, assumes that this was the house of The Haldenbys. The pottery date would be right. Hadley in his *History of Hull*, 1780, records how the famous family of Haldenby once lived in a magnificent Hall (now wholly destroyed and buried in oblivion).

The first Ordnance Survey map shows the field on which 40 West End was built, to be named Hall Close. J. G. Patton in his book *Country Independent Chapel* shows a map by Wilson-Barkworth with a plus cross and the inscription 'Site of Antiquities'. James Reckitt had conducted an excavation on the site but it is not known where, nor did he leave any records. A Mr Farmery, his gardener, worked on the site but could not remember anything being found.

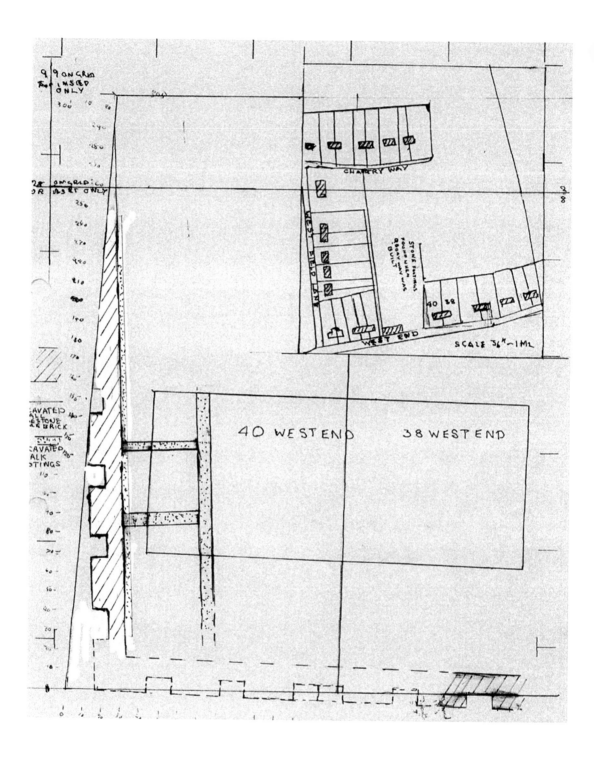

Fig. 4 Excavation Plans at 40 West End

THE LORDSHIP OF THE MANOR OF SWANLAND

The purpose of the preceding chapter has been to provide a feeling for the general nature of the medieval village. We now turn to the specific families that held the Lordship of the Manor, with a brief chronology followed by their respective histories.

Year	Lordship of the Manor

1086   **de Mortimer**

It could well be that Ralph de Mortimer's manors of Ferriby or Alvengi included Swanland and that he was thus the village's first Lord of the Manor (see the section relating to the Domesday Book). There is, however, no clear evidence of this.

1210   **de Vescy**

The first certain evidence to the Lordship comes in 1210 in the Chronicles of Meaux Abbey, which makes reference to Eustace de Vescy and "..his men of Swanneslond".

de Furnival

With the demise of the de Vescys, the Lordship passed to the de Furnivals and then by marriage to the de Usflets.

1286   **de Usflet**

By 1286 we learn that John and Loretta de Usflet are to hold the manor of the chief Lords at a rent to Gerard de Furnival during his life and subsequently free of payment.

1316   By 1316 the manor of Swanland cum Ferriby was jointly held by "the Prior of Ferriby et Lora de Usflet" (see Nomina Villarum).

1410/11   In 1410, accounts for the manor were prepared for Loretta's great grandson, Sir Gerard de Usflet. These are stated to be: "of Gerard de Usflet under the Lordship of Swanland" so at that time the manor remained with the Usflet family.

1420   Gerard de Usflet died without issue and in his will of 1420 left the manor of Swanland split between his sisters Isabelle de Usflet and Johanna Stapilton. Isabelle de Usflet married Robert Haldenby.

1492/   There exist Manor Court Rolls, (1492-1579), which connect the
1579   Haldenby and Stapilton families with the manor of Swanland

1644   The manor remained with these families until the Civil War when Robert Haldenby's lands were sequestrated as a consequence of his taking up arms on the side of King Charles against Parliament.

THE DE VESCYS

(Vescy, Vesey, Vessey, Vesci)

Swanland's association with the de Vescy family is first recorded in 1210 in which year the Chronicles of Meaux Abbey state:

> "…During the same time (the Abbey) gave to Eustace de Vescy fifteen marks, that he might confirm to us our lands at Myton as to extent, and that he might fix boundaries between our men and his men of Swanneslond, who on many occasion had taken our sheep on our pastures of Myton for debt or any other cause whatsoever. And that was done. [14]

Fields named *Vesey Flats* were still shown on the pre-enclosure map of the village as late as 1824.

The family took its name from Vassey in Normandy and had crossed to England with William the Conqueror. A Robert de Vessey is mentioned in the Domesday Book as having holdings in Leicestershire, Lincolnshire, Northhamptonshire and Warwickshire. A descendent, Ivo de Vesey, became Baron of Alnwick and by 1099 had acquired the Mortemers' manor of North Ferriby.[32] His daughter, Beatrix, married Eustace FitzJohn and brought with her estates in land, in North Ferriby and elsewhere. Their son, William, took the name of de Vescy.

In 1138, Eustace fought on the Scottish side against the English in *the Battle of the Standard*, at Cawton Moore, in Yorkshire. The Scots lost and in about 1140, as a penance for fighting on the losing side, he founded the Priory of St. Mary at North Ferriby.[32] Later he founded those of St. Mary at Malton, St. Mary at Watton and the Priory at Bridlington. The Priory at North Ferriby was built:

> " ..for his own soul and for the remission of his sins and also for the souls of his mother and father."

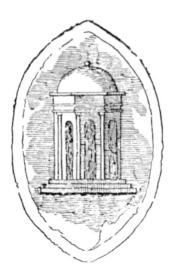

Fig. 5 The Seal of Ferriby Priory

Between 1150 and 1153, Eustace de Vescy and his wife, granted to the Nuns of Watton, ..(a villager named) Orm of Ferriby with his messuage (house), and 3 bovates (ca 45 acres) of land.[33] Between 1157 and 1170, this was confirmed by his son, William, with mention also made of Orm's wife and son.[34] People as well as land were thus conveyed from one estate to another.

By 1210, Hugo, the fifth Abbot of Meaux, was requesting a Eustace de Vescy (a later generation?) to confirm to the Abbey their lands at Myton.

In 1272, the widow of a William de Vescy presented a relative, Richard de Vescy, as Rector of North Ferriby. She also presented Rectors to that church in 1280, 1281 and 1282.

In 1297 there is reference to a licence allowing William de Vescy to transfer three bovates (ca 45 acres) of land and 30s of rent in Swanneslund and Fereby to the Prior and convent of Northferyby.[35] Whether this transfer was ever achieved appears uncertain.

We know the land holdings of the de Vescys and others in Swanland cum Ferriby around about this time from a document known as *Kirby's Inquest (1277-1295)* a survey made at the time of Edward I. An enquiry was conducted into the land and rents of those who held them immediately of the King. The names and holdings appearing for Swanlond and Swaneslund, Ferriby cum Braithwait, together with their land holdings were as follows:

Land Holdings in Swanland (1277-1295)

(A carucate of land was approximately 120 acres and
a bovate approximately 15 acres)

Name	Place	Holding	
		Carucates	Bovates
Gerard de Furnival (that of de Vescy)	Swanlond		10
	Swaneslund, Ferriby cum Braithwait		
Vesci		8	
Robert of Roos		1	
Richard of Anlaby		1	
Alanus de Coupeland			6
Petrus Devill di		—	
Willemus Smalman			3
Robertus Maresc			2
Nicholaus de Westhous			3
haeres de Captoft		—	
haeres de Brisbang			2
Loretta de Furnivale		Remainder	
Total		16	-

Loretta de Furnivale was a lady of some standing in Swanland, of whom we shall read more later.

Fourteen knights' fees were held by the heirs of William de Vescy, including Swanneslond (Swanland), Myton, Heselee, Ferby, etc.[36]

The last of the de Vescys, William of Kildare, died at the battle of Bannock Burn in 1315, leaving no issue. He had left the advowson of North Ferriby Church (the right to choose the Rector) to the Prior and brethren of the Priory.[37]

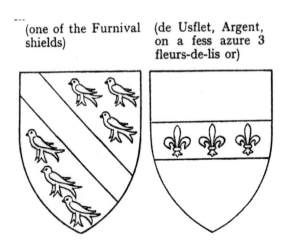

(one of the Furnival shields)   (de Usflet, Argent, on a fess azure 3 fleurs-de-lis or)

With the demise of the de Vescys, the lordship of Ferriby and Swanland passed to the de Furnivals and then by marriage to the de Usflets. At this time Edward I acquired the village of Wyke from the monks of Meaux, and granted a charter to Kingston-upon-Hull, a town which was to grow rapidly during the 14th century.

The first reference to the de Furnivals and the village comes in 1272, when a Gerard de Furnival acquired "a bovate of land and three roods of meadow in Swanland, Braythweys and Custmerche…for five marks of silver."[38] Gerard also held within the manor of Ferriby, land in Myton, which he exchanged with Robert the Abbot and the monks of Meaux Abbey for land in Braythweys between 1270 and 1280.[39] (Braythweys is Danish for a broad clearing). The de Furnivals, a wealthy family, came from Munden Furnival or Great Munden in Hertfordshire.

Gerard had a daughter and heiress, Lora or Loretta, who by 1286 had married a John de Usflet. An agreement at that time between John, son of Walter de Ousflet, Loretta his wife and Gerard de Furnival states:

> "..of the manor of Swanland ..to John and Loretta..to hold of the chief Lords at a yearly rent to Gerard during his life of 60L of silver.".

(and) "After Gerard's death the manor to be held free of payment of the said rent"[40]

Lora's husband, John de Usflet, came from the small village of Ousefleet on the south bank of the River Ouse, not far from Goole (See Fig.6). Lora's father appears to have
died between January 1293 and November 1295, when Sir John de Usflet, as he now appears, was granted free warren in the manor of Swanland.[41]

As we saw earlier, Loretta's land holdings in Swanland appear in Kirby's Inquest. The Rev David Bulman suggests that in 1293 she held seven and a half carucates or about nine hundred acres.[42] Her husband held property in Wyke-upon-Hull described as :
> " ..three plots of land for which he paid rentals totaling £1-6s-8d. The largest of these, with messuages (houses) upon it, lay near the south end of Hull Street (High Street) and extended on both sides of it, one part reaching from the street itself to the King's Quay,"[43]

In 1303 an inquiry was made into a proposal for a road to lead westward from Kingston-upon-Hull to pass through:
> "the middle of the common pasture of Miton, Feriby, Swanlund and Anglay, containing three acres and one perch",
and also:
> "through the middle of the meadow of the Lady of Swanlund, containing three roods, worth 2s".

A note attached to this second entry makes it clear that by this time Loretta was widowed.[44] She was later to have a second marriage to Sir Geoffrey de Scrope, Chief Justice of the King, Lord of Masham.

By 1315 Swanland's right of common pasture was being restricted for we read:

> "…John de Swanland, clerk, and other free tenants of the same town,claim that they and their ancestors were accustomed to have common pasture (from) the town of Swanlund to the town of Kingston-upon-Hull….from the time that memory exists, until they were hindered therein by Richard Oysel, late keeper of Kingston-upon-Hulle…"[45]

In the following year:

> "..Loretta, late wife of John de Usfleet, John Lisson, Nicholas son of John de Swanneslond and Stephen his brother..and others, broke by night the walls and dykes made for the preservation of the King's manor of Miton in Kingeston-upon-Hull and his lands, so that his corn and meadows were submerged.[46]

At that time Loretta held Swanlund cum Ferriby jointly with the Prior of Ferriby.[47]

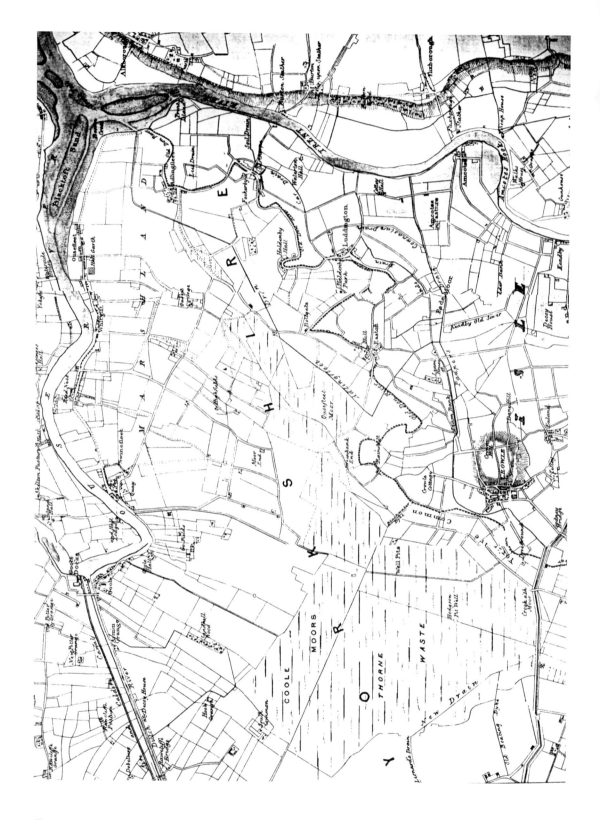

Fig. 6 Isle of Axholme showing the Villages of Ousefleet & Haldenby

In 1317, Loretta was accused of: "..a sin of the flesh with Sir William Petit, chaplain.". To be fair she did not admit to it and promised:

> "..that if I am unable to purge myself four handed with as many honest maidens, or am otherwise legitimately convicted, I will within one month pay 10 pounds sterling to be distributed in alms or for pious uses."[48]

The Lady of Swanland appears in the Lay Subsidy Assessment of 1332 (see later). This was a tax assessment based on ownership of movable goods. Those of the Lady of Swanland included wheat, barley, carthorses, oxen, sheep and a cow. The total assessment was valued at £7 9s 10d.

Loretta is believed to have had a daughter, Margery, who married Sir Hugh de Pickworth and whose effigy lies in Selby Abbey. Margery's right hand rests on the coat of arms of the Usfletes and her left hand on that of the Furnivals.

Whether Loretta's involvement in breaking the walls and dykes of the king's manor in 1316 was a response to Swanland being 'hindered' from using the common land at Myton or as some suggest, the beginnings of a dispute over the water supply from Springhead, is not clear. Certainly water became an issue. In 1293 it was reported that: "the town of Wyke was abundantly supplied with fresh water coming from Springhead,"[49] though Wyke was then only a small village. During the following century, as Kingston-upon-Hull, it grew rapidly. The building of Holy Trinity Church began in 1312, the erections of the town walls was commenced in 1322 and by 1377 its population was said to be 1557.[50] With this growth there came an increased demand for water in which both Sir Gerard de Usflet and Richard de Swanland were involved. In 1377 the mayor and burgesses of Hull :

> "made a most grievous complaint unto his majesty (Edward III) that they had no fresh water. Nor could procure any but such as was brought daily out of Lincolnshire to their exceeding great trouble..and that the neighbouring towns of Yorkshire as Hassell, Anlaby and Cottingham and others had combined together and absolutely refused to let them have any fresh water. Upon which the king issued out immediately a commission to Michael de la Pole, ..Gerard de Usflet (and others), knights, to find a speedy way to supply this town."

> As soon as the inhabitants of the aforesaid towns heard this, they made grievous complaint to the King that the taking of their fresh water..would be a ruin to their lands and goods.."[51]

A new jury was empanelled to prove the case, which they did upon oath. This included Robert de Swanland.

Fig. 7 Lady Margery Pickworth,
Believed to have been the daughter of 'The Lady of Swanland'

By 1392 there were riots by villagers following the: "taking and drawing their fresh waters from them" and in 1402 when a canal was being cut from Springhead to the town of Kingston upon Hull, villagers: "assailed the workmen and beat them from their work." The dispute was still continuing in 1412 when the mayor and burgesses requested the intervention of the Pope. The latter's response was mild but according to the eighteenth century historian, Abraham de la Pryme, he could: "nowhere find after this (that) any more troubles were acted or done."

Loretta's grandson, Sir Gerard de Usflet, knighted in 1372, undertook duties for the King such as surveyor of the riverbanks, tax collecting (1380) organizing militia (1383), sheriff (1384), commissioner of the peace (1385) and parliamentary representative in London (1400). In his will of 1405, he gave :

> " one acre of arable land at the west end of the town of Swanland to maintain for ever the light before our Lady in the chapel of Swanland."[52]

A set of accounts prepared for his son, also Gerard de Usflet, are available for the year 1410 to 1411.[53] These specify the amounts due under various headings from the townships within the manor but do not give the names of individuals. The document is headed:

> "..The account of William Freeboye, collector of rents and farm (rents) of Gerard of Ousefleet under the lordship of Swanland, from the feast of St Michael in the year of the reign of Henry IV counted the eleventh (1410), until the year of the reign of the aforesaid Henry (counted) the twelfth (1411).

The accounts give comparative figures for Swanland, Elveley, Ferriby and Hessle, and also an indication of the sort of charges levied.

The Sir Gerard, for whom these accounts were prepared is said to have fought at Agincourt with a retinue of nine lances and thirty archers. His will of 1420/21 required him to be buried in North Ferriby Priory Church.[54] He left:

> "..all his land in Swanland to be sold and distributed among the poor, and if they should extend so far, to provide services for me every year."[55]

His daughter, Isabel, married Robert Haldenby.

VILLAGE TAXES

(For a fuller account of the Lay Subsidy System see Appendix 3.)

The earliest detailed tax record for Swanland is an early 14th century manuscript relating to the so-called Lay Subsidies.[56.] The document is to be found in the National Archives, and is number 26 in Exchequer Class 179, Sub-class 202, part of the records of the King's Remembrancer or Chronicler. It is written on vellum, and is roughly 12_ inches (32 cm) square.

It was written in Swanland almost seven hundred years ago, and is therefore one of the earliest documents referring to the village. The surface of the document is somewhat abraded and the writing in many places is now quite faint. This immediately reduces the legibility of the text. The writing is a form of Old Law Hand. This was in use long before the style of handwriting commonly used in Tudor times, which is usually described as Secretary Hand. The forms of the letters of the alphabet are often very different from the standard forms we use today and indeed can vary from one clerk to another within the same period, according to the particular usage of the writer. And of course, as an official document of that time, it is written in Latin. Finally, the Latin is considerably abbreviated, especially after the first entry on the roll. For all these reasons, transcribing documents such as this into modern English is a laborious and painstaking task.

The title of the document presents comparatively little difficulty: it reads "The tax of a fifteenth of the vill of Swanlund and Bratthwatt in the year of the reign of King Edward III reckoned as the sixth". The term 'vill,' or township, is a medieval term that passed into disuse with the development of the system of local administration based on parishes. It was usually quite a small community, as indeed was Swanland. *Bratthwatt* (sic) or Braithwaite was a hamlet just to the north of Swanland, on the Raywell to Riplingham Road, now known by its later name of Braffords. Edward III came to the throne in 1327, so the sixth year of his reign was 1332. It is for the Lay Subsidy of that particular year that by far the greatest number of records still survive, so it is not surprising that the earliest known surviving document referring to Swanland is for that year. 1332 was also the last year in which a detailed breakdown was submitted, showing the assessment for each individual and how it was arrived at, rather than a simple note of the total liability of the vill. By that time, too, a distinction was made between the rural communities (the vills) which were taxed at a fifteenth and the boroughs which were taxed at a tenth; so there was something to be said for living in the country.

There then follows a list of twenty-one people in Swanland and four in Braithwaite who paid the tax.

In the left hand column we have, in each case, two abbreviations: vnd and xv. Vnd stands for *vendibiles,* meaning saleable goods, and xv, a fifteenth. There then follows an amount, being the sum of the tax to be paid. This is expressed in pounds, shillings and pence *or* (in abbreviated Latin) *libri* (li. – pounds), *solidi* (s. – shillings) and *denarii* (d. – pence).

Then comes the name of the taxpayer, followed by the abbreviation 'ht' for *habuit* (he had), then *in bonis* (in goods). After this a list of the saleable goods and their individual values, and the total value of the taxable items. It is in reading this list of names, goods and amounts, despite the difficulties of faded ink, worn paper, unfamiliar handwriting and abbreviated Latin, that the real difficulties are encountered and, indeed, a few have so far proved to be insurmountable.

Christian names, in their abbreviated Latinised forms are, in most cases, discernible, e.g. Robtus for Robertus or Robert, Ricus for Ricardus or Richard, and Petrus for Peter. Surnames, on the other hand, were only just coming into general use and not everybody had one. A man might simply be known as Peter son of Robert, though in due course this might become Robertson and be used as the *family* surname from then on. Other surnames were mostly derived from the names of occupations or places of origin. However, identifiable individuals on the Swanland list include Robert de Compland (or Coupland), Thomas Chapman, Robert de Bratthwatt, Peter de Bratthwatt, Richard de Seton and Matthew Wys(e].

The first name on the list is particularly intriguing. It simply reads "Dna de Swanland". In this context the abbreviation 'Dna' stands for 'Domina' or 'Lady', the feminine form of the common Latin noun 'Dominus' or 'Lord'.

The first entry on the list (Domina de Swanlund) is therefore a reference to the Lady of Swanland, none other than Loretta de Furnival, Lady of the Manor of Swanland at that time. Her saleable goods are listed as follows, the amounts of cereal crops being given by weight in quarters:

Nine quarters of fine wheat (*frumenti*)	worth 4s 6d per quarter,		40s	6d
Eight quarters of barley (*ordei*)	worth		36s	
Four cart horses (*affri*)	worth		20s	
Four oxen (*boves*)	worth		26s	8d
Twenty sheep (*bidentes*)	worth		20s	
One cow (*vacca*)	worth		6s	8d
Total value of goods (*summa bonorum*)			£7 9s	10d

Having goods to this value, Loretta is the most highly taxed member of the community, all other householders having saleable goods worth less than five pounds. Most of their goods fall into the categories listed above, though other commodities mentioned include oats (*avene*) and peas (*pise*), and several villagers keep goats (*capri*), and another, pigs (*porci*).

Owing to the exemption from tax of the very poorest members of the community, we have no means of knowing what proportion of the total population of the village is represented by the twenty-one households cited here. There is no reason to suppose that Swanland was relatively more or less wealthy than other small rural communities, so possibly these twenty-one households accounted for the majority of the population.

Attached to the schedule is a separate slip of paper, measuring just one and a quarter inches deep by eight and a half inches wide, which is a receipt for the sum of £4 17s. 6d, some 9s. 4d. (or 10%) short of the total due. This receipt, or acquittance, would be handed to the local (unidentified) sub-taxers when they handed over the moneys collected. It is sealed in the names of Tohm[a]s *(sic)* de Boulton and Ank[etin] Salvayn, the two men appointed by the Crown that year as Chief Tax Collectors for the East Riding of Yorkshire. It was customary to appoint two or three such officials to act jointly for each county and it was they who were ultimately answerable for the proper collection of the expected revenue.

It is particularly interesting to note that, on this occasion, charges of concealment were subsequently brought against these officers. Salvayn immediately protested that, in practice, de Boulton alone had levied and accounted for the whole sum and, finally, his colleague accepted full responsibility. [57]

The authorities first became aware of irregularities at the time of the following Lay Subsidy in 1334, when new chief taxers were appointed for the East Riding.[58] The official schedule, or county roll,[59] which had been given to the new taxers, showing what each vill had paid last time, did not tally with the receipts which were held locally.[60] The documentary evidence was laid before the barons of the exchequer who summoned the culprits to appear before them. At this point, de Boulton took pre-emptive action, and obtained a letter under the great seal, pardoning him of all wrong-doing, on condition that he answer for all the sums concealed.[61] (Then, as now, apparently, the Crown gave higher priority to the recovery of the revenue than the punishment of the transgressor).

It eventually emerged that de Boulton had pocketed a total of £80 19s 8_d, some 9% of the revenue for the entire Riding. Certainly, as indicated earlier, there is a discrepancy between the total assessment for Swanland and the amount of the receipt.

THE FAMILY de SWANLAND

The de Swanland family of the village of Swanland

The very first record to be found, relating to this family, is in the muniments in Westminster Abbey in a document from year 1282.

Taken from an extract from Roll 206 of the Pleas at Westminster:

> "….before William de Beresford and his fellow justices of the King's bench in Trinity term. 10 Edward I (*i.e. 1282*). Viz. Precipe to (Reginald de Gynges) Sheriff of Hertfordshire to summon John de Somery to answer by what services he hold his tenements of Richard de Bachesworthe in Bygrave and Denardeston (present Bygrave in Hertfordshire and Denston in Suffolk), which services the same Richard granted to Simon de Swanelonde by fine."[62]

Despite extensive research, the author of this piece can find no record of another place name that resembles "Swanland" either in England or in France and so we have chosen to believe that this man, living in the South of England, either came from Swanland in the East Riding of Yorkshire or his ancestors did. As we shall show later, there were definite links with Simon de Swanland, his heirs and other people who lived in Swanland during the same period.

After the Norman Conquest of Britain, all at the court of King William would have spoken Norman French. At this time surnames, as previously mentioned, were not in use but, as there were many people with the same first name, ways had developed to tell one "Simon" from another. In this case one's place of origin was used. Thus we have a Simon of Swanland. In French, *of* is *de* and so we have Simon de Swanland.

At this time in our history, the King and his Court would move around the country, dispensing justice in each area in turn. Meticulous records were kept of each transaction. For example the Patent (i.e. open) Rolls were public records of royal letters and decrees; the Close (i.e. closed) Rolls were records of grants from the crown which were not for public inspection; the Fines referred to land transactions; the Inquisitions were ecclesiastical records or records of the king's investigations. It is from these and similar records that most of the information has been found about the de Swanlands.

We know that one branch of the family lived in this area as it is recorded in the Patent Rolls of 28th July 1315, and again on 20th February and 10th October the following year, that "Loretta, late the wife of John de Usflet, John his son, Gerard de Usflet, Nicholas son of John de Swanneslond and Stephen his brother, …. (6 others)

...,William Bradan of Westlevele (Westella), John Bradan of Westelvele and others broke by night the walls and dykes made for the preservation of the king's manor of Miton in Kyngeston-upon-Hull and of his lands there, so that his corn and meadows were submerged". [63]

On 3rd July 1301, John de Swanland and two others were fined ten shillings for an assault on Richard de Anlaby.[64] The animosity between these families obviously continued as, in 1311, there was a complaint to the courts "... by Stephen, son of John de Swanland that Richard de Anelauby of Westelvelage (Westella), with others, assaulted him at Westelvelage co. York, and at Swanland, in the same county, carried away his goods."[64a] He too was fined ten shillings.

In 1320 Nicholas de Swanland held land in Monkgate (now called Blackfriargate), Hull and in his will of 1342 he bequeathed it to his son, Robert, who sold the tenement (property) – by now divided into two - in 1352.[65] North Ferriby Church holds records of the death of Nicholas, son of John of Swanland, in 1342 and Patton notes that, "He bequeathd his best animal for his mortuary."

It is recorded in 1329 that "Walter, Prior of North Ferriby, claimed against John de Swannesland, clerk, messuage, 102 acres of land and 12 acres of meadow in Swannesland, as the right of her Church".[66]

On 12th June 1333 Thomas de Swanlund, citizen of London, owed £50 to the Archbishop of York for lands in Yorkshire. Was he a wool farmer here? On 4th. January 1338 an order was made:

> "to permit Thomas de Swanlond, citizen of London, to take ten sacks of wool to that city, as it was ordained in Parliament at Westminster on Monday after St. Matthew last, that no-one of England, Ireland, Wales or Scotland within the king's power, except kings, queens and their children, should use cloth which was bought after the Michaelmas following."[67]

In the turbulent times in which the de Swanlands lived, the kings needed men to fight for them and one way was to give people a pardon for crimes committed, in return for their service to the king.[68] In 1339, Richard de Swanland was granted pardon (together with others) for the death of William de Peder of Beverley.[69]

On 18th July 1352, there is a record that "Robert, son of Nicholas, son of John of Swanland conveyed 2 messuages (plots) of land in Oldfre Lane (also now believed to be Blackfriargate) to John de Upsalc" and in 1365 a document in the Yorkshire Fines[70] shows William de Swanlond and his wife Joan owning land in Hull which they had "to hold (for) Robert and his heirs".

We find another connection with the de Swanlands and the church in the Patent Rolls of 12th May 1390, when it is recorded that a chaplain is appointed to Layerthorpebrigg, York, by the resignation of Nicholas de Swanland. Again, on 4th April 1396:

> "Licence for Nicholas Swanland and Robert Halton, chaplains, to found a chantry of one chaplain in the church of St. Peter 'in les Willoghes' in Walmegate, York, with the assent of Thomas, Archbishop of York, the prior and convent of the Holy Trinity, who hold the church to their own uses, and the parishioners of the said church; and to erect houses and buildings on certain parcels of land in divers parts of the cemetery of the church ......(full details of positions and measurement)....and to alienate the premises in mortmain to the chaplain of the chantry and his successors celebrating divine services four days a week in the said church for the good estate of the said Nicholas and Robert, while living, and for their souls after death and the souls of their ancestors and benefactors. For 1 mark paid in the hanaper."

As evidence that the de Swanlands in the Hull area and those in London and North Mimms are of the same family, we use several sources.

An entry in the Fines of 1329 records:

> "...from John de Swanland, clerk, to John Bradan of Swanland, one messuage of 70 acres of land and 4 acres of meadow in Swanlund. To hold to John Bradan for life; remainder to Richard, his son and his heirs".

Richard Bradan appears often, both in documents and as a witness to documents signed by Simon, from 1322 to 1333.[71] In the Westminster Abbey Muniments there is a document, dated 1332, showing Simon granting land in North Mimms to Richard and on 18th October 1332, he witnesses a document where Simon is now the Lord of Herefeld. We also have documents showing a grant in 1330 to a "William Bradan of Swanneslond".[72]

The last mention found of Richard Bradan is referred to in the taxation of the "Vill of Swanland and Brathwatt" for 6th year of the reign of Edward III (1332). People were then taxed on their saleable goods at the rate of 1/15 and Richard possessed "4 quarters of fine wheat and 4 quarters of barley, 36s; 3 cart horses, 15s ; 3 quarters of peas, 9s 6d and other goods totalling 75s.[72a]

In 1331 we discover a John de Swanlond, clerk, who is "owed money from the late king for goods bought for his wardrobe". This John was a relative of William of Melton (Archbishop of York 1317 to 1340) and brother to Simon of Swanland, *the king's merchant from Hull,* who acted as banker to William Melton.

An entry in the Close Rolls at Westminster on 10th June 1344 record, "Simon de Swanlund, knight, and Simon, his son, acknowledge that they owe to John de Flete and John, son of Nicholas de Swanland in the county of York, £54 10s to be levied of their lands and chattels in the city of London."

In the National Archives in London there is a document that is a writ from Edward III dated 8th February 1369 regarding land holdings in Swanland.[73] It mentions Cecilia, former wife of John, son of Richard of Swanland. A preliminary translation is included in Appendix 10.

The Borthwick Institute at the University of York holds the will of Elizabeth, wife of Thomas de Swanland, draper of Beverley dated 9th April 1404. A translation is also included in Appendix 4.

We think of flyposting being a modern inconvenience but, on 5th July 1408, the Provost of Beverley complained of "notices being posted to the contempt of the king" and the list of those responsible included one Thomas Swanland. He was in trouble again two years later when Thomas, Bishop of Durham, complained that he (plus 17 other named people) "broke into his close at Walkyngton in the county of York, depastured his grass and coppice there with beasts and assaulted and ill treated his servants..."

The last mention we have found of a member of the local de Swanland family is in a book by Stannywell held in Kingston upon Hull archives, referring to a Thomas Swanland (and three others) buying land in Munkgate from John Bilton, draper, on 30th April 1429 and, on 27th October 1438, they "sold a messuage and shops in Marketgate at the north east corner of Holy Trinity churchyard and a tenement in Munkgate to William Sharp and John Dodyngton".

During the research on the de Swanland family much information has been discovered about members living in other parts of the country plus some details on named individual members where their residence was not clear. As this book is on the history of the village of Swanland, a list of references to other de Swanlands has been included in Appendix 13, at the end of this volume.

THE COUNTY OF KINGSTON UPON HULL

In the year 1440, King Henry VI granted a new charter to the town of Kingston upon Hull, which brought the course of the fresh-water dyke from Anlaby within its jurisdiction.

In 1447, he:

> "..confirmed his former grants of the towns being a county town and having a county belonging thereto totally distinct and separate from the county of York."[74] and the county of Kingston upon Hull was thus formed.

Swanland, as well as the villages of North Ferriby, Kirkella, Westella, Willerby, Haltemprice, Wolfreton, Tranby, Anlaby and Hessle were then brought within its boundaries (See Fig 8). Part of the parishes of North Ferriby and Hessle were already in the town and it was thought that it was right for these to be entirely within its jurisdiction.[75] Swanland and Tranby were townships within the two parishes.

Two significant consequences resulted. Firstly:

> "..all writs briefs, warrants, praecepts, &c for any within the town and ye new made county [would] be executed by the proper officers of the said town of Kingston upon Hull."[76]

In other words Swanland came under the jurisdiction of Hull. Secondly:

> "..the mayor and burgesses of the same town and their successors for ever [could] dig wells and springs anywhere within ye county of the said town."[77]

The county, empowered by this charter, purchased Julian and Derringham Springs from Anlaby and cut a new dyke, Spring Dyke, to convey fresh water to Hull.

The boundaries of Hull were not to be altered again until 1832, when a new parliamentary borough was created.

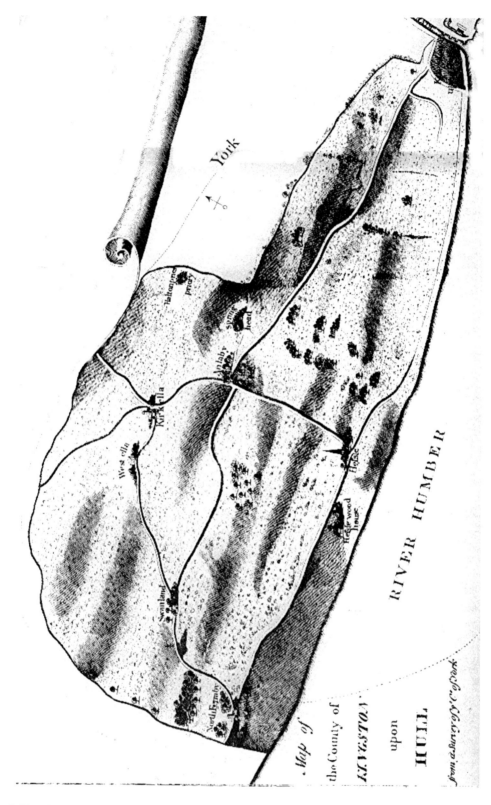

Fig. 8 The County of Kingston upon Hull, (Hargrave 1791)

48

THE TUDOR AND STUART PERIODS

TIMELINE

Swanland		The Nation	
1410	Mention of Robert Haldenby in the Minister's Accounts for Swanland		
		War of the Roses	1455-1485
1485	Three men sent from Swanland to Leicester to assist Richard III		
		As the 16th century opened, Life expectancy was 30-35 years, with luxuries such as sugar, alcohol, pepper, oranges and books in short supply	1480-1520
		Martin Luther, the founder of Protestantism, nails his thesis to the church door at Wittenberg	1517
1492-1579	Mention of Haldenby and Stapelton in Manor Court Roll for Swanland	Elizabeth I accedes to the throne	1558
		The Pilgrim Fathers fled religious persecution by sailing to found a Colony in America	1620
		The principal battle of the English Civil War at Marston Moor	1644
1646	Robert Haldenby was "in arms against Parliament."		
		The Toleration Act established freedom of worship	1689
1693	The Independent Chapel is built		
End of 17th C.	Money raised for the defence of the realm:		
	Hull	£6538	
	Swanland	£541	
	N.Ferriby	£261	

THE HALDENBYS OF SWANLAND AND HALDENBY

The Haldenbys, the Stapletons and the Manor of Swanland

It will be remembered that Isabelle de Usflet married Robert Haldenby. The manor of Swanland was held by the Haldenby family, jointly with the Stapletons, from 1421 to 1640. Little has been found connecting Stapletons with the village in the form of rentals, but there is in Newby Hall a record of a fine levied between Francis G (H)unter, plaintiff, and Robert Stapleton Kt., deforciant, concerning cottages and lands in the manor of Swanland and fishing rights in the Humber. There is also recorded in books by Tildall Wildbidge[78] and by Rev. J.G. Patton[79] that a Mr Haldenby was the largest contributor in Swanland to the Exchequer of James I who ruled from 1603-1625. The Haldenbys tenure is reputed to have ended in 1641. (The date of the contribution quoted by Tildall Widbridge of 1662 must be incorrect.)

The Haldenbys' Hall

Hadley in his *History of Hull, 1791*[80] talks of the famous family of Haldenby or Holdenby living in a magnificent Hall, which he says is "now wholly destroyed and buried in oblivion". Although no evidence can be found to link a Haldenby residence to Swanland, the Rev. J.G. Patton[81] states that an old map in the Wilson Barkworth Collection shows a large plus cross in a field that is aptly named Hall Close. This field is adjacent to the field that contained the Chapel of Ease and/or Chantry. Is this a coincidence?

There are clues that link Hall Close with the Haldenbys in the form of archaeological evidence. In the corner of the writer's property at 40 West End as previously discussed there is a seven foot thick foundation of a buttressed wall. Several archaeologists have examined this and agree that this must form part of a precinct wall that was perhaps defensive. During the building of Queensbury Way the writer was asked to inspect masonry that was being exposed and recorded that the wall continued for sixty yards behind 40 West End. In several of the gardens of Queensbury Way other masonry, such as steps, have been found. There are other pieces of limestone wall to be found in the village that, in most cases, form boundary walls, possibly built from stone recovered from the Hall. Very little dating evidence has been unearthed but the pottery shards found date to the sixteenth century.

Because of this evidence, the writer considers it fair to assume that the remains in West End are part of the Hall belonging to the Haldenbys, Lords of the Manor of Swanland. It stands at the highest end of what was the village main street, and the road changes direction to run parallel to the front wall.

The Origin and Lineage of the Haldenby Family

The Haldenby family originated in the village or hamlet of Haldenby. This lies at the junction of the rivers Trent and Ouse on the south side of the latter, close to the village of Whitgift (Fig. 6). As has been mentioned in the history of the Usflet family, the Haldenby connection with Swanland started when Robert Haldenby's wife, formerly Isabelle de Usfleet, together with her sister Johanna Stapilton, inherited the Manor of Swanland from her brother Sir Gerard de Usfleet. Sir Gerard de Usfleet died without issue and, in his will of 12th February 1420, he left the manor of Swanland split between his sisters. Sir Gerard had fought at the battle of Agincourt together with his retinue of nine lances and thirty six archers.[82]

Robert Haldenby made his will on 4th November 1452 and his wife died about the same time. His son John married Isabell daughter of Justice Portington.[83] Nothing is recorded for several generations. Descendents were as follows. John and Isabell, (who died intestate 7th December 1453) whose son, another Robert, married Elizabeth, daughter of William Scargill of Thorpe. Her sister married Robert Legard of Anlaby. The next Haldenby in line was another John who married Kateren, daughter of Sir Robert Helyard. Their son Robert married Anne, daughter of Sir Guy Dawney of Koyke. The sequence changes here as they named their son Robert after his father. Robert married another Anne, daughter of Thomas Boynton of Holderness.

Their son and heir was named Francis and he married Elizabeth, daughter of Sir John Wentworth of Emswel. Elizabeth died in 1562 and was buried in North Ferriby Church. Hadley, in his History of Hull, 1788,[84] tells of a picture of a lady kneeling with her four sons behind her and an inscription in Latin which when translated reads:

> " pray for the soul of Elizabeth Haldenby…the wife [of]… Esqs….and the daughter of John Wentworth who had thirteen sons…which soul God required, 1562."

Many people have thought that this was a picture on a wall but on Francis Haldenby's tomb in Adlingfleet Church there is a picture sculpted into the side. This depicts a man kneeling on one side and a lady on the other with their family behind them on each side. No doubt this is the type of picture Hadley was describing.

The Haldenby Coat of Arms

At this point it is interesting to look at the family blazon or coat of arms for the Haldenby family. Up to the 1st December 1563 their shield had been quartered eight ways,[85] including the shields of :

      1. Haldenby, 2. Gawtree, 3. Usfleet, 4. Furnival
and on the second row:
      5. Ferriby, 6. Luddington, 7. Ella, 8. Wentworth

In heraldry "Quartering" means dividing up, not necessarily into four. At this time Francis and his brother Robert were uncertain of their family's arms and were being pressed by the new Protestants to change their blazon. On the helm (helmet) there was a crest depicting a bent arm with a fist clasping a chalice. Their motto was: "The Divine Toast". This apparently offended the Protestant Church so the complete arms were changed. There were now only six quarterings and the crest became a black swan holding a twig of laurel, no doubt with Swanland in mind. In heraldic language the blazon reads

      1. Vert, a fesse between two cups covered or.
      2. Paly of six argent and azure, on a chief gules a lion passant or.
      3. Argent on a bend sable three lions passant gardant of the first.
      4. Argent, a chevron between three boars heads couped azure.
      5. Argent on a fesse azure three fleurs–de- lis or.
      6. Argent, on a bend 6 marteletts gules.

The crest is on a torce, or and vert, a swan sable, beaked and membered gules, holding in its mouth a laurel slip vert.

The grant is titled "Francis and Robert Haldenby. This was granted by William Flower alias Norry, King of Arms". (An example with the correct tinctures can be seen on the front cover, some heraldic explanations are given in appendix 11.)

There is an anomaly here. Francis died in 1596 and had been granted a new blazon in 1563 yet his tomb in the church at Adlingfleet still bore the original arms. Was this pure defiance of Catholicism or was it that when his wife died in 1562 he had two tombs made together? It would appear from description that they were similar.

The tomb at Adlingfleet has an effigy of Francis on its lid. He is lying with his head resting on his helm, clearly showing the chalice and the arm. On the coffin side there is a picture carved in stone of a figure kneeling with his hands clasped in prayer. Behind him is a retinue of kneeling children, twelve in all. It would appear that the man is taking communion and the children are waiting for hands on blessing. On the sides are two small shields one with the arms of the family Wentworth the other for Haldenby. Fastened into the wall above the tomb is a plaque with the last messages from the children, written in Latin. The church conveniently provides a translation. One wonders why this tomb is in Adlingfleet and where the tomb of his wife is now. Is it lost because the church in Ferriby objected to the strong Catholic symbolism?

Fig. 9 Effigy of Francis Haldenby
The name of each person is sculpted into the ribbon below their feet

Returning to the family lineage, Francis and Elizabeth's son and heir was Robert who married Ellenor Tywitt. Robert died before his father but his son, also Francis was born in 1572. This Francis went on to marry Elizabeth Darley and they produced a son, also Robert, who married Jane Cobb of Ottringham. This Robert died in 1641 when his son, yet another Robert, was very young, (approximately 15 years old) and had appointed Sir Francis Cobb to be the young man's guardian.

Young Robert, who was eighteen in 1644, took up arms on the side of King Charles against Parliament, classifying him as a "delinquent". The King was defeated at Oxford during the time of Robert's service. At the time of the surrender it was said that Robert had neither taken oath nor covenant. In other words he remained a Catholic.

To quote from the Composition papers:[86]

> "He is seized in lands at Swinefleete and in two third parts of the manor of Haldenby with a windmill and other lands in Adlingfleet and in two thirds of the passadge of Barton Stather ferry and two third parts of land in Swanland with a yearly value of £161-1s. There will come to him after the decease of Jane Haldenby, his Mother and of Elizabeth Haldenby, his Grandmother, all lands in the aforesaid towns worth yearly £136.10s.4d.10 Dec 1646"

The death of Elizabeth is recorded as 6th November 1654.[87] She must have been aged 82. It is recorded that Robert, who was a sufferer in the Royal cause, lived at Swanland or Beswick and was buried at Kildwick on the Wolds on the 19th August, 1656. He had married Katherine, daughter of Sir Thomas Knollys. She secondly married Thomas Keithtly of Sherriff Hutton in 1658. Robert only had sisters, (four), so the line became extinct after his death at the age of thirty.

SWANLAND AND NATIONAL EVENTS, 1348 – 1690

The Plague

The Plague or Black death first appeared in England in 1348 and there is mention of:

> " …the circuit of (Hull's)walls being incomplete when the pestilence of 1349 killed a great part of its inhabitants."[88]

Hadley[89] describes a further visitation of the plague to Hull in 1472 where it raged until 1478, leading to the deaths of many of the inhabitants. Others fled the town in order to escape and it became almost derelict. There were later outbreaks in Hull in 1576 and 1635 and in Beverley in 1604.[90]

Local villages such as Riplingham are known to have been affected. Swanland was very small, less than 35 households, and it may be supposed that in the countryside, where both the human and rat populations were less dense, the effect was less severe. Nevertheless, a few miles from Hull at Meaux Abbey, there were 49 monks and lay brothers before the pestilence of 1349 and only 10 when it had ceased and on the opposite side of the Humber, Barrow needed three new vicars in one year. Life in Swanland would certainly be affected adversely by the demise of Hull.

The War of the Roses and Richard III

In 1447 the County of Kingston upon Hull was established which included Swanland. There is evidence that men from the county, and at times specifically from Ferriby cum Swanland, were involved in events of national importance, including the War of the Roses and the subsequent conflict between Richard III and Henry Tudor.

In the War of the Roses in 1461, Edward IV of the House of York deposed Henry VI of the House of Lancaster and assumed the throne. It is recorded that the Prior of North Ferriby gave six quarters of malt to provision Edward's ships. In 1469 there was a rising in Yorkshire against the new king led by Robert Hillyard (Robin of Holderness). This was put down but twenty men were sent from Hull and twelve from the County of Hull to assist in suppressing a further rising.

In 1470 Henry VI was restored to the throne. Edward fled to France but returned with an army in 1471 and reclaimed the crown. When yet a further Lancastrian rebellion occurred in the north, the town and county of Kingston upon Hull was required to provide and equip thirty armed men to assist in putting it down

In 1481 armed men were raised to serve against the Scots. Eight came from the county. They were paid about a shilling for thirty four days.

In 1483 Edward IV died and his young son, also Edward, succeeded to the throne. But by October, Edward V had disappeared, probably murdered, and Richard, Duke of Gloucester, The Lord Protector, was proclaimed King. There was a rebellion by Buckingham at Leicester and Richard ordered as many armed men as possible to join him to put it down. Three of these came from Ferriby with Swanland.[91] A further fourteen came from Hull, four from Hessle, and three from Kirkella, Anlaby and district.

The East Riding Muster Roll

Swanland is mentioned at the end of the 16th century in the East Riding Muster Roll. This was a list of the number of men each town/township was expected to provide in defence of the shire under an Act of 1554. Renton Heathcote compares the number of armsbearers from various towns and villagers in the area as follows:[92]

Arms bearers at the End of the 16th Century

Town/Township	Armsbearers
Hull	719
Beverley	451
Hessell	69
Anlabie	43
Swanland	38
Willerbie	31
Ferrebie	22
Kirkie Elleye	19
West Ellie	10
Woolferton	5

The Defence of the Realm

An Act of Parliament was passed in 1690 to establish a defence budget and money was raised based on property values. Assessments of rents in the county of Kingston upon Hull were listed as follows:

Rental Assessments for the Defence of the Realm[93]

Town/Township	Rents	
	£	s
Hessle	831	0
Anlaby and Wolfreton	616	0
Swanland	549	10
Kirk Ella	297	10
Ferriby	261	0
Willerby	196	10
West Ella	114	6

References

1. J. G. Patton, *A Country Independent Chapel,*
    A. Brown & Sons, 1943, p16
2. John Nicholson, *Place Names of the East Riding,*
    Transactions of The East Riding Antiquarian Society, Vol XXV, p106.
3. A.H.Smith, *The Place-Names of the East Riding of Yorkshire and York,*
    Cambridge, Cambridge Press, 1937, p218.
4   Thomas Thompson, F.S.A., *Researches into the History of Welton and its*
    Neighbourhood, Kingston-upon-Hull, Leng & Co.,1870, p181.
5. G.N.Garmonsway, *The Anglo Saxon Chronicle,*
    London, J.M.Dent & Sons Ltd., p204.
6. Ibid, p205.
7. Ibid, p143
8. Rev D.J.Bulman, *North Ferriby, A Villagers' History,*
    Lockington Publishing Co.1982, p9.
9. Encomium Emmae, p 8.
10. J.G.Patton, Op cit. p16
11. Harl 1394, p217.
12. Elizabeth Hallam, *Domesday,* Public Record Office, 2000, pps 4,5.
13. William Farrar, Hon.D.Lit., Early Torkshire Charters VolII,
    Edinburgh,Vallantine, Hanson &Co, 1916
14. Thomas de Burton, Abbot, *Chronicles of Meaux up to the Year 1396,*
    (Hull Local Studies Library).
15. A.B.Wilson-Barkworth, *The Composition of the Saxon Hundred*
    in which Hull and Neighbourhood were Situate,
    Hull & London, A.Brown & Sons.
16. A.B.Wilson-Barkworth, *Domesday Book for the East Riding of Yorkshire,*
    Scarborough, W.H.Smith &Son, 1925.
17 Thomas Gent, *History of Hull,*
    Hull, M.C.Pack & Son, 1735 reprinted 1869, pps. 3,4.
18. Rev D.J.Bulman, Op.Cit.,p12
19. *The Great Roll of the Pipe for the 34th Year of King Henry II,*
    London, The Hereford Times Ltd.,1925
20. G.Collier, *The Lay Subsidy Assessment for Swanland 1332,*
    A Transcription from the East Riding Lay Subsidy Assessment of 1332.
21. *Hearth Tax,* Lady Day 1672, Public Record Office,E179/205/504
22. J.Norden, *The Surveyors Dialogue,* 1607.
23. D.Hey [Ed], *The Oxford Companion to Local and Family History* (Oxford 1996), p310
24. M.Ellis, *Using Manorial Records ,*(PRO Publication 1994), pp10-11.
25. Ibid. p16
26. Ibid pp 11-13.
27. Ibid pp 52-55
28. West Yorkshire Document, No WYL5013/2592
29. West Yorkshire Document, No WYL5013/2612
30. M.Ellis, *Using Manorial Records,* PRO Publication 1994.
31. Humberside Archaeological Partnership.
32. The Rev. D.J.Bulman, Op.Cit. p18
33. Early Yorkshire Charter, 1107

34.   Ibid. 1195
35.   Calendar of Patent Rolls Ed.I, 29th June 1297.
36.   Yorkshire Inquisitions, (1304), Vol. IV, p 67.
37.   The Rev. David Bulman, Op.Cit.p19.
38.   Yorkshire Fines 1272-1300. Vol.CXXI, 4, Ed.I
39.   A.W.Richardson, Yorkshire Archaeological Journal, Vol. XXXVIII, p 255.
40.   Yorkshire Fines, 1272-1300, Vol CXXI,16, 1286.
41.   A.W.Richardson, Op.Cit., p255
42.   Rev, D.J.Bulman, Op.Cit., p25
43   A.W.Richardson, Op.Cit., p254
44.   Yorkshire Inquisitions, Vol. 4,
45.   Calendar of Patent Rolls, Ed.II, 16th April, 1315.
46.   Calendar of Patent Rolls, Ed.II, 10th October, 1316.
47.   Kirby's Inquest for Yorkshire, Surtees Society, Vol. 49, Footnote
48.   Rev. D.J.Bulman, Op. Cit., p23
49.   Renton Heathcote, *Anlaby, The History of an East Yorkshire Village,*
        Beagle Publications,1999, p27
50.   Renton HeathcoteIbid, p28.
51.   Abraham de la Pryme, *A History of Kingston upon Hull, ca.1700,*
        Kingston upon Hull City Council & Malet Lambert High School, 1986, p11
52.   Rev. D.J.Bulman, Op.Cit., p26.
53.   G. Collier, *Ministers Accounts for Gerard of Ousefleet,1410-1411,*
        West Yorkshire Archive Document No.WYL 5013/2589. A Transcription.
54.   A.W.Richardson, Op. Cit., Pedigree of the Second House of Furnival.
55.   Rev. D.J.Bulman, Op.Cit. p26.
56.   Lay Subsidy Rolls E179/202/26, The National Archives.
57.   J.F.Willard, *Parliamentary Taxes on Personal Property 1290 to 1394,*
        Mediaeval Academy of America, Cambridge, Mass.1943, p189.
58.   Ibid. p215
59.   Lay Subsidy E179/202/18, The National Archives.
60.   Lay Subsidy E179/202/16, E179/202/19, The National Archives
61.   Calendar of Patent Rolls, 1334-1338, 175.
62.   Westminster Abbey Muniments # 4740
63.   Patent Rolls
64.   Patent Rolls
64a   Patent Rolls, Edward II, 6th July 1311
65.   East Riding Archives Vol. 8
66.   Patton J.G., *A Country Independent Chapel, p4*
67.   Patent Rolls
68.   see appendix 14, Thomas de Swanland
69.   Patent Rolls
70.   1347-1377 Vol L11
71   Westminster Abbey Muniments # 4122, 4155, 4156, 4189, 4318, 4324, 4325, 4399, 4425
72   Westminster Abbey Muniments # 4157
72a.   National Archives, E 179/202/26
73.   National Archives ref. C202/167/18
74.   Abraham de la Pryme, Op.Cit., p26.
75.   Victoria County History, East Riding of Yorkshire, Vol?, p4
76.   Abraham de la Pryme, Op.Cit., p26.
77.   Ibid., p27.
78.   Patton J.G. *A Country Independent Chapel* p18
79   Ibid p18
80   Hadley History of Hull, p849.

81   Patton Ibid p8

82   Yorkshire Archaeological Journal Vol XXXVIII, p258.

83   John Haldenby Married Isabelle Portington ibid Y A J

84   Hadley History of Hull, p849

85   Haldenby Coat of Arms

86   Royalist Composition Papers II Vol XVIII, p140

87   East Riding Archives PE 36/2

88   Hadley George Hiistory of Hull, p65.

89   Ibid, p65

90   Renton Heathcote Anlaby The History of an East Yorkshire Village, p88

91   McMahon History of Hull BB3AF, p135

92   Renton Heathcote Ibid, p86.

93   Ibid, p87.

THE CHURCHES OF SWANLAND

INTRODUCTION

Swanland was not recognised as a separate parish by the Church of England until 1997, when the village acquired its own vicar who worked independently of North Ferriby. The absence of the established church in the village has led to an unusual history of worship. A nonconformist chapel, now Christ Church was established at the end of the seventeenth century and this provided a centre for worship in the village, and the village school. The history of this school is described in volume 2 of *A New History of Swanland.*

A minister, Rev. John Whitehead, collected the nonconformist Independent Chapel's history at the end of the nineteenth century but this was not published. The present author has had access to his manuscript on which much of this section is based.

In 1828, a Primitive Methodist Chapel was built and this maintained a separate congregation until 1981 when the congregation joined those who worshipped at Christ Church. The Wesleyan Methodists had a separate congregation for a period during the nineteenth century but no building.

Until 1899, members of the Anglican Church walked or travelled by carriage to North Ferriby for their services. However the twentieth century saw the opening of an Anglican mission hall in the village, managed by North Ferriby parish. This subsequently became St. Barnabas Church.

BEGINNINGS OF CHRISTIANITY IN EAST YORKSHIRE

Saint Paulinus and King Edwin

The first written account relating to early Christianity in the country was completed by Bede in 731. This is entitled *A History of the English Church and People.*[1] Bede spent his life in a monastery in Jarrow and many of his writings are centred on the north of England and, as the events relating to East Yorkshire occurred only some hundred years before Bede finished his history, his account should have some authenticity.

King Edwin, son of King Ella who gave his name to Kirkella and Westella, in 616 defeated in battle and killed Aethelfrith, the rival king of the north and thus became king of the whole of Northumbria, from the Humber to the Tweed. He was at this time a pagan.

Fig. 10 Mound of King Edwin's castle
in the grounds of Aldby Park, Buttercrambe near Stamford Bridge, Yorkshire

This was the era of the establishment of Roman Christianity in the south of England, as brought by Augustine and forty monks from Pope Gregory in Rome. King Edwin married Ethelberga who was a Christian and daughter of King Ethelbert of Kent.

King Edwin gave assurance that his wife would be allowed to practise her religion and she came north with her spiritual adviser, Paulinus.[2]

Paulinus was consecrated bishop in 625 and he was determined to bring the Christian message to the people of Northumbria. Bede states that once he had entered Northumbria he worked to maintain the faith of the companions who had accompanied him from Kent and if possible to bring some of the native heathens:

"to grace and faith by his teaching"[2]

The king allowed his daughter to be baptised in the Christian faith after her birth on Easter Day, when the king had survived an attack by an assassin sent by the king of the west Saxons. Thus the scene was set for Edwin's own Christian baptism and he and many of his chief men finally became Christian, following much thought about the teachings of the faith and discussion with Paulinus. Edwin was also influenced by a vision which he had received before he defeated Aethelfrith. His chief priest in the pagan religion, Coifi, destroyed the idols, altars and shrines that had been used for worship of their pagan gods and became a Christian. His figure is represented on the reredos of Beverley Minster, next to that of Paulinus. This destruction of temple and contents occurred at Goodmanham in 627.[3] The king and many of his subjects were baptised in York on Easter Day 627 at the church of Saint Peter the Apostle,[3] originally built in wood and subsequently enlarged by King Edwin.

Fig. 11 The present church,
probably on the site of the pagan temple at Goodmanham

Following the king's baptism, Paulinus, who had been consecrated as Bishop of York, continued preaching round the kingdom and baptised many people in the Christian faith. James, the Deacon, continued his work when Paulinus returned to the south of England.

Another holy man has local associations, namely John of Beverley. He established a monastery at Beverley and had many miraculous cures attributed to him. After bishoprics in Hexham and York he finally resigned in 717 and spent the last four years of his life back in peace in the monastery in Beverley.

Although this account of Christianity in East Yorkshire has started in 627 during the Anglo Saxon period, there is no evidence to suggest that the faith did not arrive here earlier, particularly during the Roman occupation. It is known that many Romans accepted Christianity and that they were very close to Swanland, at Brough (Petuaria). Indeed remnants of a Roman road were excavated at Melton Quarry[4] so the possibility of Roman occupation near the village is feasible. What was their religion? Bede gives little detail about Christianity in the Roman period save the mention of Saint Alban's martyrdom in 301. The arrival of Christianity in East Yorkshire during that period is mere speculation. What is known, is that the incursion of the Angles and Saxons during the fifth century virtually removed Christianity from England, so the country was ideal for conversion at the time of Saint Augustine's arrival.

FERRIBY PRIORY AND PARISH CHURCH AND SWANLAND CHANTRY

Between the eighth century and the time of the Norman conquest in the eleventh century, the Church was established throughout England with the familiar pattern of parishes and dioceses. Domesday Book, 1086,[5] contains an entry for North Ferriby stating:

> "A priest is there and a church"

North Ferriby church served Swanland and North Ferriby for many centuries until around 1900.

In 1140, according to Tanner,[6] a priory was founded at North Ferriby by Eustace, husband of Beatrice de Vescy (see section on the de Vescy family). The canons at the priory provided hospitality to the pilgrims travelling to Beverley to Saint John's shrine.[7] From 1295, the prior and brethren were permitted to choose a rector for the parish church and eventually they were able to receive the income of the rectory and appoint a vicar to serve the parish and its church. This was one of the canons who had care for the spiritual needs of the chapelries at Swanland and St. Mary's Lowgate, as well as the chantry at Melton.[8]

There has been much speculation about the position of the chapelry in Swanland but the most favoured site is in the vicinity of Chantry Way. Patton[9] states that records of noted Swanland families, such as Todd and Watson, contain references to this chantry. The Ordnance Survey map of 1888 shows ruins of a chapel opposite Westfield Farm just north of the modern Chantry Way. One piece of evidence for this site was the discovery in 1942 of a lead Bulla* of Pope Clement III (1187-1191) by Mr J. R. Lewis in his garden in Chantry Way.[10]

Fig. 12 The Bulla, currently displayed in Swanland Primary School

* A Bulla is a seal of lead, hardened perhaps with a little silver, that was always attached to Papal Bulls and other documents issued by the Vatican.

These chapels or chantries were subsidiary places of worship served by a chaplain. The origin of the one in Swanland is unclear. A document written in 1332 by the Archbishop of York (William de Melton) states that the vicar of North Ferriby shall:

> "at his costs find one chaplain to celebrate thrice a week in the chapel at Swanland, and shall find and sustain that chantry as the rector of the church of North Ferriby was heretofore accustomed to do."[11]

Sir Gerard Usflete's will of 1405[12] states that an acre of arable land at the west end of Swanland should be given to pay for the maintenance of a light before our Lady, in the Chapel of Swanland.

In 1444 John Brompton, a merchant of Beverley, in a codicil to his will gave for:

> "the building and adornment …. of the Chapel of Swanland 3s 4d etc"[13]

In 1481 Richard Kirkman of Swanland left in his will half a quarter of malt:

> "to the chapel of the Blessed Marie of Swanland".[14]

Thus the name of the chapel is known and there is documentary evidence for the existence of the chapel.

The chapel at Swanland was therefore a chantry, which was a chapel built or endowed by an individual to ensure the singing therein of masses for his or her soul. No record exists as to who this individual may have been. The chantries were suppressed by Henry VIII and Edward VI, between 1545 and 1547. However, in 1569 Gyles Baynes, curate of North Ferriby, presented York with a bill for nine years' unpaid expenses:

> "Item, for the said Gyles Baynes his waiges for bringe the Cure iij tymes in the weike at a Chappell called Swanland beinge bound by composition thereunto eache yere. During ix yeres o-iiij[li] in toto xxxvj[li]," (9 years £4. Total £36).[15]

The 'cure' is the cure (or care) of souls, being the origin of the word curate.

It is not known how long the chapel was used or stood but tradition has it that the Dissenters, who finally built the chapel by the pond, used Swanland chantry until 1693.[10] Villagers would have to walk to North Ferriby church for services when the chantry was no longer functioning. North Ferriby and Swanland Parish
At the time of the Reformation in England monasteries and priories were dissolved by an Act of Parliament in 1536. The priory at North Ferriby was therefore

disbanded and a priest would be appointed by the diocese to administer the Church and chapels in the parish. The present Church building in North Ferriby was first used in 1848 but several structures probably existed in previous centuries.

Fig. 13 North Ferriby Parish Church, 2004

In the building standing at the beginning of the nineteenth century:

"the chapel on the north side of the chancel was the burying place of the famous family of Haldenby, who lived in a magnificent hall at Swanland; ....There was a picture of a lady of that family kneeling with four sons behind her, and the following broken and imperfect inscription, with three coats of arms:

> Orate pro anima Elizabethae Haldenbi, ...Uxorem ... Armigerumm ... et filiam Johannes Wentworth, qui tredecim habituit filias et eid ...quam animam Deus condonat, 1562."[16]

> (Pray for the soul of Elizabeth Haldenby, ... wife of ... Esquire, and daughter of John Wentworth, who had 13 daughters and ... whose soul may the Lord pardon 1562.)

There were also two testamentary burials where the will directed burial in the church itself for notable residents of Swanland:

1342   Nicholas, son of John of Swanland. (see also p 44)
1452   Robert Haldenby

In the period following the Reformation, churchwardens, overseers of the poor and surveyors, who were all local people, helped the vicar in running the parish and maintaining the church. As village life was still so closely bound to the church, the responsibilities of these officers often extended to the lives and welfare of the villagers. The Church book entries[17] for the 1690s show the responsibilities of people in Swanland as well as North Ferriby.

"April 14, 1691 Overseers for the Poor of the Town of Ferriby for the year ensuing are William Thornton and John Onyon. For Swanland Robert Mush jun. and Richard Elliott. Overseers of the Highwayes for Ferriby John Feild and Francis Akam. For Swanland Robert Coulson and Peter Burrell.

March 29, 1692 (Saturday before Palm Sunday)
    Overseers for the Poor ......For Swanland Peter Burrell and Richard
    Elliott. Highwayes....For Swanland ... John Turner and John Jefferson
    jun.

April 10, 1694 (Easter Saturday)
    Overseers for the Highwayes .... For Swanland are Peter Acy and
    Samuel Newton. Overseers for the Poor ... For Swanland ... Robert
    Parker and Christopher Boynton.

March 16, 1695 (Wednesday after Easter?)
    Overseers for the Poor ... For Swanland Peter Acy(crossed
    out)Benjamin Galland and John Akam. Overseers for the highwayes
    Henry Watson and Benjamin Galland."

The Church Books give details of the poor rates contributed by residents of the two villages. For 1662, it is interesting to note that several of the wealthier ratepayers lived in Swanland, from which 41 contributions were made. The highest contributor was Robert Galland who paid fifteen shillings (75p).

Of interest are some of the answers given to Archbishop Herring's enquiry in 1743.[18] At this time William Huntington was vicar of Kirkella and this parish included responsibility for North Ferriby and Swanland with its own. This lasted from 1663 to 1766. William Huntington's reply indicated that there was a total of about sixty households in the two villages and about half of these worshipped at the Presbyterian Meeting House in Swanland. This perhaps explains the absence of a resident vicar in North Ferriby in addition to the statement in the return that:

"the Vicarage House being come down"

The dissenting Presbyterians assembled in their Meeting House known as the Independent Chapel, in Swanland:

"twice every Sunday from several Towns in the Neighbourhood to the number of two hundred or upwards and are taught by one Mr John Anger(sic)."[18]

The history of this chapel is described in a later section.

It is said that in the middle of the eighteenth century Church life was:

"formal, pedestrian and prosaic, but it was not dead"[19]

This was the era of John Wesley and other reformers who had congregations ready to receive new forms of worship. Methodism came to Swanland in 1828, as described later.

THE INDEPENDENT CHAPEL IN SWANLAND

Background

The seventeenth century in England was no less dramatic in the religious world than the sixteenth had been through the arrival of the Reformation. There were now many different sorts of Christians and the Commonwealth period, from 1649 to 1660 when the monarchy was restored, was one of great turmoil and unrest. Following the restoration it was hoped by Parliament that some uniformity could be developed within the established church of the country, namely the Church of England, which had the King as its 'supreme governor'. In 1662 a new Act of Uniformity was passed in which it was stated that church services were to be conducted according to a revised prayer book and liturgy. This directive caused the compulsory resignation of about 2000 clergy throughout the country, some of whom were from East Yorkshire. The most relevant to Swanland's story was John Ryther who was minister of Bromby and Frodlingham in Lincolnshire and came to settle in Brough.[20] He probably did some preaching in the district before moving to London and could have influenced the views of local people. There would also have been influence from the neighbouring vicar of Rowley, who had nonconformist views and eventually went to America.

A minister, who had probably had a greater influence on the foundation of the Independent Chapel in Swanland, was the Rev. Samuel Charles who had been expelled from the Presbyterian Chapel in Bowlalley Lane in Hull in 1683, settled in Welton, and travelled up and down the Wolds countryside preaching and speaking in farmhouses and elsewhere.[21] The Swanland Presbyterian congregation was listed amongst Yorkshire congregations in 1688.[22] This connects with the use of the former chantry by the dissenters, until 1693. The right of nonconformist groups to worship had been suspended in 1662 by the Act of Uniformity but renewed by the Toleration Act in 1689.

As described previously, there was no established church in Swanland so this would be a village to which these travelling preachers would have come to introduce their versions of Christianity. The local people must have been inspired by the visitors for one of their number, William Shaw:

> "sold for 5/- the land whereon the chapel stood, empowering certain persons to receive from the congregation the annual rent of one peppercorn."

This statement comes from the deed of the original chapel, dated 6th William III (i.e. 1693).

Although the original dissenting group that had been meeting in Swanland adhered to the Presbyterian code, the fact that the chapel was known as the Independent Chapel indicates that the congregation belonged to the Independent nonconformist sect that rejected both episcopacy and Presbyterianism. They would have believed in the autonomy of local church congregations and most were deemed Congregationalists. This was the version of nonconformism followed in Swanland chapel.

Development of the Building

The first building was completed in 1693 and the chapel and adjoining school were established for worship and education of the residents of Swanland, Ferriby, Anlaby, Hessle, Kirkella, Willerby, Melton and Elloughton. There are three long-standing accounts of the early history of the chapel.[23,24,24a] All these have drawn on the research undertaken in 1899 by the Reverend J. E. Whitehead[25] and on the autobiography written by Thomas Blossom, in 1847.[26]

As already stated, the land on which the chapel by the pond now stands, was conveyed by William Shaw, Yeoman. The Shaw family must have played an important role in the life of the chapel. Joseph Shaw had preached in Swanland in the middle of the seventeenth century. During the eighteenth century, in 1740, Nathaniel and Thomas Shaw are listed as Trustees.[27]

Thomas Blossom, in 1777,[26] wrote:

> "Swanland is a village that has long been favoured with the preaching of the gospel. It appears that a Mr Shaw, one of the ejected ministers in the reign of Charles II, settled at Swanland, where a Dissenting Chapel was built and where some of his descendants remain to this day"

The original chapel was designed to house 450 people, a number which seems large by today's standards. Amongst the original thirteen trustees of the chapel are names which have become familiar in Swanland's history: William Watson, gentleman, Thomas Pickering, carpenter, Henry Watson, yeoman and John Turner, yeoman.[25]

In 1696, John Turner conveyed some land to the chapel to enable a minister's house to be built.[28] This house still stands in West End and is now called 'The Old Parsonage'. This land abutted grounds of John Turner to the south and Sir Griffith Boynton, Bart. to the west. Later, in 1855, the east end of this building was rebuilt and heightened by another storey. John Todd, Senior, of Swanland Hall paid for this. By 1939 the old manse had become damp and a new one, now Hillcroft, in Westfield Lane was acquired. The Moderator of the North East Province described this as "the finest in Yorkshire". John Turner was also Overseer for the Poor in Swanland in 1692.[17]

Fig. 15 The Old Parsonage, West End
A photograph taken early 20th century

The original chapel building must have decayed considerably during the eighteenth century, for in 1803 a new chapel was built, which is substantially the one seen today, although the two porches were added in 1840 through a generous donation from John Todd of Tranby Park. The first schoolroom which was attached to the north side of the chapel was not replaced until 1854.[29] By then it was described as dilapidated and:

> ".....a building of two storeys, cottage like in appearance, the upper
> storey being the schoolroom and the lower the vestry. Both had
> direct communication with the chapel."

James Watson, Esquire, of Swanland Manor offered to build, at his own cost, a new schoolroom and vestry in two wings on either side of the 1803 chapel. These are the two side pavilions to be seen today. These new wings were opened in 1854 after the death of their donor, on 11th December 1853.

Fig. 16 The Independent Chapel, late 19th century
with Priory Farm on the left

Fig. 17 Christ Church, 2004
with the Institute and Mere Way development on the left

In 1881 extensive improvements were made to the interior of the chapel. These included:

erection of a communion platform;
carpeting and refurnishing, including cushions for pews on ground floor;
addition of a baptismal font and flagon with plates for communion, as gift from the pastor (Reverend J.E. Whitehead);
alterations to the pulpit and addition of a wall behind the pulpit, bearing the text 'Enter into His Courts with Praise';
conversion of front seats into choir stalls with space for harmonium;
provision of lamps for Evening Service, a gift from John Shaw of Beech Hill.[30]

Fig. 18 Interior of the Independent Chapel
c. 1881, before 1928 alterations

Fig. 19 Interior of Christ Church, 2003
showing the structural alterations

1893 saw further renovations to commemorate the bicentenary of the chapel's foundation and in memory of Eliza Todd who died in 1892. This memorial was funded by John Todd, her brother, and included repair to the window frames and roof and a new heating apparatus. There was a memorial inscription which read:

> "By her death the chapel and its minister lost their best friend and helper. Her memory will be engraved upon the hearts of all who knew her"

There were also gifts from prominent members of the congregation. These included an American organ from Sir James Reckitt, Bart. of Swanland Manor. This replaced the harmonium which was moved into the vestry. Mrs Duncan of Swanland House gave a pulpit bible and hymnbook in memory of Andrew Duncan, a trustee, who had died earlier in the year.[31]

1928 saw further internal alterations to cater for the fashions of the twentieth century.[32] All the box pews were replaced by the current Austrian oak ones. The Westerdale family paid for the pulpit apse. The Blossom family donated the pulpit and Mrs Whitehead and her daughters donated the communion table and chairs. This work was supervised and partly undertaken by Mr Louis Calvert who was a Chapel Deacon at the time.

Later in the twentieth century, roofing repairs were undertaken, a crèche was added and the north vestry extended. New lavatories were built and an extra room behind the pulpit added. Finally, in 2000, extensive refurbishment occurred in the balcony. The church was redecorated in authentic Georgian décor.[33]

Fig. 20 The balcony in 2003, after the refurbishment

This account of structural alterations to the chapel building through the centuries shows some significant facts about its successive congregations. There is frequent mention of donations from the members and a desire to maintain the fabric of the building, showing a great loyalty and affection for it and their faith. Many of the donors have been wealthy landowners or businessmen of the village and further consideration will be given to some of these later in this account.

The chapel has separate entrances for the downstairs and the balcony. In the days when class distinction was so prevalent, the downstairs was reserved for the gentry – hence the cushioned seats mentioned in 1881 – while the farming folk worshipped from the balcony. Evidence of this was found in the 2000 balcony renovation when removal of the floorboards showed several inches of soil from the boots of those who walked around the fields and dirt track roads. There were also several artefacts discovered including a child's well-chewed kid glove, a first catechism belonging to Martha Carlill, dated June 7, 1825, a New Testament, a scent bottle stopper and an 1888 newspaper.[33]

Fig. 21 Plaque to commemorate 300 years of worship at Christ Church

Gifts of Sacred Vessels

Gifts of Sacred Vessels

During the early years of the chapel's existence the community was acquiring silverware to enable its members to celebrate Holy Communion. In 1723 a solid silver cup was presented:

> "The gift of Thomas Watson to ye Dissenting Congregation in Swanland, 1723"[34]

In 1789, another solid silver cup "For the Lord's Supper" was a bequest to the Protestant dissenting congregation in Swanland, from Jeremiah Turner of Anlaby.

Fig. 22 Communion Silver

Chapel Deeds, Trustees and Ancient Payments

There have been at least four sets of deeds drawn up for the chapel and many sets of trustees over its three-century history. Familiar Swanland names are evident amongst the trustees and also names from neighbouring villages. The original list reads:

William Watson	Gent	Swanland
Thomas Pickering	Carpenter	Swanland
Henry Watson	Yeoman	Swanland
John Turner	Yeoman	Swanland
John Ellyot	Yeoman	Anlaby
Edmund Ellerker	Yeoman	Anlaby
Thomas Penrose	Yeoman	Hessle
Francis Hunt	Yeoman	Hessle
William Thornton	Yeoman	Ferriby
William Thornton, Jr	Yeoman	Melton
Francis Carlill	Yeoman	Elloughton
Thos. Marshall	Husbandman	Kirk Ella
John Rispin		Willerby

Signed by William Shaw

By 1740 the trustees included Thomas Todd. The Todd, Watson and Shaw names continue to run through until the start of the twentieth century.

In 1876, the new school building by the pond was opened, as described in volume 2 of *A New History of Swanland*, and the school was the responsibility of the chapel for a number of years. This necessitated conveyance of the school site to the trustees in 1881. In addition to the responsibilities associated with the school, the trustees also had oversight of the charity established by Jeremiah Turner in 1789. The will stated that £600 should be invested for the benefit of the minister and £200 for the schoolmaster.[34] The will also provided a silver cup (already mentioned) and *apparently* a house for the schoolmaster. This last bequest was subsequently declared null and void in 1796, through the Statute of Mortmain.* The lack of provision of a schoolhouse was to have repercussions in appointment of schoolmasters in later years.

*Statute of Mortmain, 1279. This limited grants of land to the church in consequence of the loss of feudal benefits, originally held by the church, to lay lords.

On a tablet near the pulpit, during the pastorate of Mr Whitehead, a number of ancient payments to the chapel are recorded. These are from the local landowners and farmers and most amount to £1 or less per annum. The schoolmaster, Mr Witty, heard from his predecessor, during the last part of the nineteenth century, that other payments had existed from as far away as Sancton, Cottingham and Beverley.[35] This gives an indication of the large area served by the chapel.

In 1852, John Todd, formerly of Tranby Park, made a settlement of £2000 for the benefit of the minister of Swanland Chapel. This had arisen from the bequest to Reverend David Williams in 1827.

The Ministers

The first minister was Emanuel Dewsnop. There is a stone on the south side of the vestry of Ferriby church with inscription:

> "Here lyeth the body of Anna the daughter of Emanuel Dewsnop sometime minister of the gospel in Swanland and Mercy his wife who died Oct 16th 1702. The small and great are there"

but no information is available about Emanuel.[36] A list of ministers through the centuries is included as an appendix.[37]

Fig. 23 Gravestone of Anna Dewsnop

Three ministers are prominent in this list, probably partly because of their long tenure at Swanland but also because of the work they did and the written descriptions they left about life in the chapel. The first of these was Reverend David Williams who was minister from 1786 until 1827.

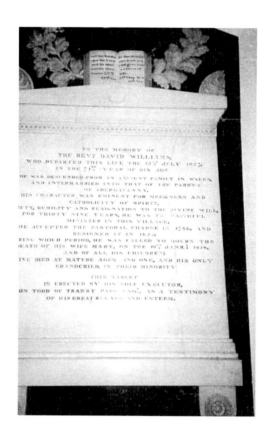

Fig. 24 Tablet in memory of Reverend David Williams erected by John Todd of Tranby Park

David Williams was obviously a much loved and respected pastor, as described on the memorial plaque erected by John Todd of Tranby Park, Hessle. This plaque is still on the wall of the chapel. It is probably through his inspiration that the Sunday School was started at the chapel in 1798. This is described later. Also during his pastorate the new chapel building was erected.

The second minister, about whom there is significant information, was Reverend John E. Whitehead who was pastor from 1872 until 1899. It is to him that a debt is owed for researching and recording the earlier history of the chapel. Through his diligence and thoroughness in searching for information and keeping written records during his pastorate, it has been possible to write a full account of the chapel's history. He was minister when the new school was built and will have had to support the head teacher during times of great change in education. His written remarks show the great concern he had for his congregation and its spiritual and physical well being.

Fig. 25 Reverend John E. Whitehead

The third pastor to mention is Reverend John Patton, minister from 1929 to 1946. He was another historian who published the history under the title "A Country Independent Chapel". He was also pastor during times of great change and anxiety in the country, the General Strike and the Second World War, so will have to have dealt with the problems encountered by his congregation.

Fig. 26 Reverend John Patton

The Congregation

From its inception the chapel has catered for people who lived in many of the surrounding villages as well as Swanland. This meant that, although most of the congregations were farmers, initially working the strips of land around the villages and later the enclosed land, there was always a good support from the gentry and landowners for the chapel. It is inevitable that more detail of the lives of the better off should appear in any surviving written documentation, although the baptismal, marriage and burial records contain the names of the farming population. The original chapel being built to house 450 worshippers must have been filled each Sunday with agricultural workers and tradesmen, all of whom will have walked, sometimes many miles, to Sunday service. The gentry and landowners must have arrived by carriage. It is known that the second chapel has separate entrances for the balcony and downstairs and that the gentry and well to do stayed downstairs whilst the others climbed the stairs to the balcony, for services.

In 1743, Archbishop Herring's Enquiry sent a questionnaire to the clergy of the parish churches. One question was "How many dissenters are there in the parish?" The reply indicated that there were three score, that is half the combined population of Swanland and Ferriby and that most of the residents of Swanland attended the Independent Chapel which had up to 200 people attending. It is this type of statement that makes one feel that the people of Swanland supported the nearest church and it is certainly true that most of the landowners in the nineteenth century were worshippers there.

In 1851, a census was taken of religious worship throughout the country.[38] The entry for the Independent Chapel in Swanland on 30th March 1851 records an attendance of 200 at the morning service, 180 at the afternoon service and 23 at the Sunday school. The average attendance over 12 weeks is given as 200 and 27 at the Sunday school. A comment at the end of the entry from the deacon at North Ferriby suggests that the attendance may have fallen during the previous two years owing to the absence of a permanent minister.

The lists of Trustees between 1694 and 1900 show members of several families that are known to have owned big houses in or around the village. The Watson family eventually built Swanland Manor in 1848 and feature in trustee lists from 1694 to 1881. The Todd family, who bought Swanland Hall in 1830, played an active role in the life of the chapel throughout the nineteenth century. It has been said of the Todds that they regarded the chapel as their private one.[39] Reverend Whitehead, whose pastorate overlapped with the successful period of the Todd family, records in his comments that the family had considerable controlling influence over the chapel's affairs, even though no member was in membership of the church. There was evidence that other leading families also stood aloof from church membership at that time. Nevertheless the Todd family was very generous towards the chapel and school and records show that they contributed when need was there.[40] The Todd regime in the chapel lasted for nearly 200 years and with the deaths of Eliza Todd in 1893, and Mr and Mrs John Todd in 1895, Reverend Whitehead stated that the deaths:

> "were everywhere keenly deplored – the village and chapel alike suffering great loss"

The Shaw and Ringrose families were also chapelgoers and landowners. When James Reckitt (later Sir James) moved into Swanland Manor in 1884 he also became a worshipper at Swanland Chapel, even though he was nominally a Quaker and attended his own Meeting House on Sunday morning. During his life in Swanland Manor Sir James made many gifts to the chapel and in 1923 the Congregational rally was held in the grounds of Swanland Manor.[41]

An account of the congregation members would be incomplete without mention of Richard Witty, the schoolmaster. He acted as clerk to the church from 1843 to 1892 and was also an acting deacon.[42]

One of the early developments associated with the chapel was the formation of the first Sunday school in the Hull and District Sunday School Union.[43] This was started in 1798 as part of the nationwide movement initiated by Robert Raikes from Gloucester. The first meeting on 15th April drew 70 scholars under the supervision of Reverend David Williams, assisted by several influential individuals. The Todd and Watson families supported the venture financially.[44] Thomas Blossom (whose life is documented in volume 1 of *A New History of Swanland*) is thought to have been of great assistance to the minister in the work of the Sunday School.[45] The Sunday School continued for two centuries and to celebrate its 150th anniversary in 1948, a leaflet was produced by Rev. D. Trevor Roberts and a celebration was held.[46]

Fig. 27 Collage made to commemorate 200 years of the Sunday School

The chapel has a central position in the village by the pond and, from accounts written by its ministers, has also played a central role in the lives of the villagers. The trustees, appointed from chapel members, ran the only school in the village for many years and, until the arrival of the Methodists in 1828, this was the only place of worship within the village. It is not surprising that Archbishop Herring's enquiry of 1743 found that nearly all Swanland's residents attended the chapel, although those who travelled from the neighbouring villages must have augmented the number of worshippers. Today it still functions as a meeting point for various groups and plays a valuable function in the village's life

Code of Worship

As has already been stated, the form of worship followed by the ministers and congregation of the chapel has been contentious from its formation in 1693. The concerns of Reverend Whitehead, late in the 19th century, about the type of religion practised in the chapel are documented in his history manuscript. He was concerned that the chapel did not seem to be adhering closely to the tenets of congregationalism and this dichotomy of practice seems to have been a feature throughout its history. During the 18th century a group seceded from the main body of the congregation and started to worship in a cottage situated on the south side of Main Street. The cottage was subsequently knocked down in 1907 and replaced by four cottages of model architecture. The split concerned the worshippers' belief in the doctrine of the Trinity. This was the time of the spread of Unitarianism and the current minister was tending towards this belief. The group of seceders returned to worship in the main chapel in 1803 when the new building was finished, under the ministry of Reverend Williams.[47]

Fig. 28 Cottages on Main Street with porches
are the ones that it is believed were used by seceders in 18th century. James
Reckitt replaced them in 19th C with two pairs of semi-detached houses

Throughout the 19th century the clergy of the chapel expressed their concern that, although the chapel was full at services with attendances approaching 200, there were never more than 25 members eligible to attend the meetings. This concern became so great in 1840 that 10 members from the congregation stated:

> "That considering the laxed state of the Church it now be dissolved with a view to its reorganization and greater prosperity"

A group formed and agreed:

> "to devote themselves afresh to the Redeemer and his cause and to strive together in prayer and effort for each others' spiritual good and the conversion of others"[48]

Reverend Whitehead comments that throughout the history of the chapel there had always been a congregation of many denominations, which included Congregationalists, Baptists, Methodists, Quakers, and churchmen meeting for worship without much practice of any distinctive type of Christianity. This possibly was because of the position of the chapel.

By 1900, the chapel was firmly associated with the Congregational Church and entries are found in returns and articles of Congregationalism relating to Swanland Chapel. The twentieth century brought the Ecumenical Movement, a revised approach to religion and ultimately falling numbers in congregations for all denominations. In 1972, the Congregationalists and the Presbyterians joined to form one church known as the United Reformed Church. This would not have affected Swanland immediately as there was no Presbyterian church with which to join but national administration must have had some impact. During the 1970s the numbers at the Methodist Church in the village became very small and in 1981 the Methodists joined the other nonconformists in the village to form Christ Church, a truly ecumenical church by the pond. A full account of the 'coming together' is to be found in the pamphlet produced about the history of Christ Church.[23] Today the minister may be from either church and the services follow traditions from all three churches.

THE PRIMITIVE METHODIST CHAPEL

Methodism in England originated at Oxford University in 1729 from a society known as the "Holy Club". The principal members of this club were John and Charles Wesley and George Whitefield. It is however John Wesley's name which is primarily associated with Methodism. The Wesleys were born in Epworth, Lincolnshire in the first decade of the eighteenth century and both were ordained Anglican priests. John started to preach his brand of Anglicanism in the churches but his evangelical approach caused hysteria amongst the congregations so that he was excluded from many churches. However he continued preaching in this evangelical manner round the countryside. He concentrated on those sections of society that he felt were neglected by the Church of England and emphasised the importance of individual salvation and the love of God. By 1784, John Wesley had established an annual conference of Methodists as a corporate body within the Church of England. The final break was made in 1795, from which date the sacraments were administered in all Methodist chapels. Methodism was, and still is, very strong in the Hull area.

Following the break from the established church, there were several other schisms, one of these was the formation of the Primitive Methodists in 1810. It was this group which built a chapel in Swanland in 1828 on land donated by Mr H. Sykes.[49] The original cost was estimated as £98[38] and the debt on the chapel at finish of building was £70.

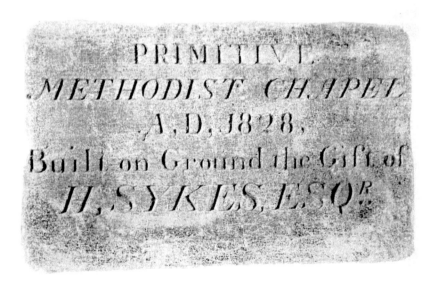

Fig. 29 Foundation stone of Primitive Methodist Chapel
now located in the balcony of Christ Church

The chapel was situated behind the village store in Main Street and was used until the mid 1970s when dwindling congregations and decay of the building caused the worshippers to seek alternative accommodation for services. Initially they used the old St. Barnabas Church (see later description), then the Independent Chapel,[50] uniting for worship with the congregation by the pond, in 1981.[23]

Fig. 30 The Primitive Methodist Chapel in 1984
from Swanland: Recollections of Life by J. and C. A. Wheeler

The census of religious worship, taken in 1851,[38] records that the chapel contained 27 free sittings and 73 sittings in pews. There was one service, held on Sunday evenings, at which the average attendance was 60, and 40 people attended for the weekday service. The total income and expenditure for the previous year had been £4 15s 4d.

Study of the Trustee minutes books[51] shows that early in the 1900s the chapel building had become unsatisfactory and discussion was made about the building of a new chapel. Land was acquired but no building was undertaken, probably owing to lack of available funds. Several renovations to the existing chapel were made, the first in 1903 after which there was a reopening service followed by a public tea. In 1929 electric light was added and new carpets were laid, this coinciding with the centenary of the chapel's building. In 1936 a new organ was installed, paid for mainly by Mr John Kirby, and a dedication service for this and new hymnbooks was held in 1937. Two years later Mr Kirby tendered his resignation from the positions of secretary and chapel steward, owing to his age and health. He had 60 years of membership.

A report of a joint meeting with the Great Thornton Street circuit officials in 1937[52] gave the average attendance at the Sunday afternoon service as 16 and in the evening as 20; 11 scholars were attending the Sunday School; £4 had been sent to the Quarter Day; collections averaged 7s on Sunday; the chapel had no debt and had money in hand in a Trust; £12 10s was received annually from the Reckitt Trust.

The Trustee minutes' books show that further alterations and repair work were undertaken in 1958 and 1960 and that by 1962 only one service at 2.30 pm was recommended for the winter months. Events taking place for chapel members, documented in the minutes, include many sales of work for money raising purposes, annual anniversary meetings and garden parties.

By 1963, discussion had started about joining with the Congregational Church[51] but the decision at this time was to maintain the status quo. The size of the collections and small numbers in the congregation must have initiated these discussions, which continued intermittently for another eighteen years. By 1975 the Methodists had decided to use the first St. Barnabas' church building for their services and subsequently, in 1981, they joined the congregation of the United Reformed church by the pond for combined worship.

In 1968, Mrs Dyson wrote an account of life in the village, as she recalled it, around 1918.[53] One chapter is devoted to the Primitive Methodist chapel. She writes about the situation of the chapel as being:

> "built in between the Butcher's shop and a row of cottages, with the lane
> in between leading to the slaughter house"

and comments that it did seem a strange place to build a chapel.

Her description gives an impression of an active church community, giving much support to its members. She describes mission and "Christian Endeavour" meetings and chapel teas for the scholars. By that time there was a Sunday school at the chapel[54] although none was mentioned in the 1851 census. There was an anniversary service once a year for the children and the numbers who came were so large that alternative space had to be found in William Andrew's cleared joiners' shop, lying on the other side of Main Street.[55] Louis Calvert carried out internal alterations in this chapel, described as a cosy place of worship, as well as at the Congregational one.[54]

Mrs Dyson had copies of class tickets belonging to the Dyson family, dated 1860 and 1870

Fig. 31 Class Tickets for 1860 and 1870

SWANLAND WESLEYAN METHODISTS

There was also a separate group of Methodists, following the Wesleyan tradition, worshipping in Swanland during the nineteenth century. The census for 1851[38] records that this group met in a hired hall, unspecified but also used for other purposes. There were 60 free seats and attendance averaged 40 at the weekly evening service. Appointment of the preachers was with the Reverend Charles Prest of Storey Street, Hull. Wm. Hy. Walmsley, tenant, completed the return. Little further information is available about this group, no mention of it being found in a statistical survey, of 1887, made of Wesleyan Methodism in Hull and district.[56] Nationally, the Wesleyan Methodists united with the Primitive Methodists in 1932, to form the Methodist Church of Great Britain.

ANGLICAN CHURCH MISSION HALL AND ST. BARNABAS CHURCH

In 1899, a mission hall was built in Swanland, on land now occupied by Wingfield House, Main Street, to serve the Church of England members living in the village.[57] This land was given to the Church by Mr Wingfield Todd.

Fig. 32 Foundation stone from original St. Barnabas Church now located by the steps to the new vicarage

For many years the mission hall in Swanland was regarded as an adjunct to North Ferriby Church. Business and decisions relating to it were made in North Ferriby and Swanland remained part of North Ferriby Parish until 1997. As the 20th century progressed, Swanland began to assume more responsibility for running St. Barnabas, particularly after a team vicar was appointed in 1984.[58]

In the early part of the century, Church Council minutes for North Ferriby Church and Service Books for Swanland mission hall/church from 1916 give a record of worship by Anglicans in Swanland.[59,60] Until 1921 services in Swanland were conducted by a lay reader, there being two Evensong services a week. There was a brief period of closure, following the departure of the lay reader but in 1923 the church was reopened and dedicated to St. Barnabas; weekly Evensong, taken by the vicar of North Ferriby, recommenced. However after this date a lay reader was still appointed for Swanland and Evensong services held, with celebration of Holy Communion once a month. Numbers of worshippers recorded for 1925 are between 12 and 26 for Holy Communion and 55 on Easter Day in 1927. By the end of the

1950s there were two services every Sunday, Holy Communion and Evensong probably reflecting the growth in population numbers in the village.

Fig. 33 Interior of original St. Barnabas Church

In September 1959, a new organ was dedicated and opened formally. This organ had come from the workhouse chapel of the Western General Hospital, Hull and replaced the harmonium. It was rebuilt in the church and an electric motor fitted. At this service, for the first time, the choir of three ladies and one gentleman wore robes of cassock and surplice.

From the 1960s a curate of North Ferriby church, with particular responsibility for Swanland was appointed and, from the mid sixties, lived in Dower Rise. The first holder of this post was Ron Dalton and later Peter Gregory who was the first curate to live in Swanland. Another curate was Allen Bagshawe, and in 1979 Mike Lowe was appointed curate and subsequently became team vicar. In 1965, a church hall was built behind the old St. Barnabas building. Sunday schools took place weekly.

Other events, which are recorded, are Harvest and Flower Festivals and, by 1971, there were three services each Sunday: Holy Communion, Morning Prayer and Evensong. Attendances were recorded as around 35 for Holy Communion and 30 for Morning Prayer.

On 8th July 1972, the first wedding was celebrated in the church, the bride being Jane Waters and the groom Robert Baker.[61]

Fig. 34 Wedding of Jane Waters and Robert Baker

The 1970s, 80s and 90s saw great expansion of the village and it was soon apparent that the original mission hall had become too small for the congregation's needs. In November 1990, the Parochial Church Council of North Ferriby and Swanland gave the go-ahead for the building of a new church. A plot of land became available as a field below Beech Hill was approved for residential development and building commenced in 1991. The vicar, Reverend Richard Hill[62] describes the raising of necessary funds as a "faith project", all money being prayed in. The new church finally opened in 1992 and was dedicated by Donald Snelgrove, Bishop of Hull on February 22nd.

Fig. 35 Dedication stone of new St. Barnabas Church

Fig. 36 The modern St. Barnabas Church on Main Street

The new church includes an electric, computerised organ and an advanced sound system, which incorporates a loop system for the hard of hearing and a relay into the crèche, lounge and other rooms. The chapel's baptistry allows for baptisms by total immersion and there is comfortable seating and specially designed carpeting. At night the cross in the illuminated chapel window shines down Main Street.

Fig. 37 Interior of St. Barnabas Church, 2004

Today St. Barnabas Church's congregation is very active and the weekly newsletter and monthly Parish magazine detail many events occurring weekly or less frequently. It became a flagship church for Alpha courses, following the movement started by Nicky Gumbel in London in the 1980s. The parishioners have constant contact with, and provide support for, people working in the Third World. There is a permanent Youth Worker for the young people of the parish. Small groups of parishioners meet regularly in homes for prayer and Christian reflection. The building provides a much-needed meeting point in the village for various groups, and concerts are often held in the church.

Although one place of worship has been lost to the village with the demolition of the Primitive Methodist Chapel, there is still much Christian activity here and the two churches play an important part in the lives of many residents.

References for Churches

1. Bede, *A History of the English Church and People,* Penguin Classics
2. Bede, op.cit., p115.
3. Bede, op. cit., p128.
4. *Roman road at Melton Quarry.*
5. *Domesday Book*
6. *North Ferriby A Villagers' History* compiled by Rev David Bulman, 1982, Lockington Publishing Company.
7. *North Ferriby A Villagers' History* compiled by Rev David Bulman, 1982, Lockington Publishing Company, p29.
8. *North Ferriby,* op. cit., p30
9. J G Patton, *A Country Independent Chapel,* (A Brown and Sons Ltd., 1942), p20.
10. J G Patton, op. cit., p21
11. *North Ferriby,* op. cit., p33
12. *See Appendix 9*
13. *North Ferriby,* op. cit., p33
14. Borthwick Institute, Wills 5/109. *See also Appendix 8*
15. Borthwick Institute, CP 1431 (*North Ferriby* p33)
16. Allen, *History of Yorkshire,* iv, p 174f
17. North Ferriby Church books, East Riding of Yorkshire Archives, Beverley
18. Archbishop Herring's Enquiry, 1743
19. J.R.H. Moorman, *History of the Church of England,* p 288
20. Edward Cookson, *Ejected Ministers of Yorkshire,* alphabetical list.
21. A.E.Trout, *Notes on East Riding Congregationalism*, from Hull and East Riding Congregational Magazine, 1930.
22. Cole, MSS British Museum, 1944.
23. Raymond Taylor and John White, *Christ Church Swanland, United Reformed/Methodist,* 2002.
24. J. G. Patton, *A Country Independent Chapel,* (A Brown and Sons Ltd., 1942)
24a A.E.Trout, Swanland Congregational Church and its History, parts 1 and 2. Hull and East Riding Congregational Magazine ,1930
25. J. E. Whitehead, Manuscript History contained in the Church Minute book. Derived from: Memorial Hall Library, London; Dr Williams Library, Gordon Square, London; British Museum; County and Local Histories; Old numbers of Evangelical and other magazines; Parish registers and deeds.
26. Thomas Blossom, *Autobiography.*
27. J. E. Whitehead, ibid.
28. Printed records of the Todd family.
29. J. E. Whitehead, ibid.
30. J. E. Whitehead, ibid.
31. J. E. Whitehead, ibid.
32. Raymond Taylor, ibid.
33. Swanland Village Association News, Summer 2000, p3.
34. J. E. Whitehead, ibid.
35. J. E. Whitehead, ibid.
36. J. E. Whitehead, ibid.
37. A. J. Trout, ibid. and Raymond Taylor and John White, ibid.
38. Census of Religious Worship, Borthwick Institue: Texts and Calendars 25.
39. J. E. Whitehead, ibid.
40. School Managers' Minutes Book, I 05/06/1889.
41. Minutes of Church Meetings, June 1923.

42. J. G. Patton, op. cit. p54.

43. *The Mayflower*, Magazine of the East Riding Congregational Church.

44. J. E. Whitehead, ibid.

45. J. G. Patton, op. cit. p36.

46. Minutes of meetings of Sunday school teachers.

47. J. E. Whitehead, ibid.

48. Minutes of meetings of Church Members, July 1840.

49. Foundation stone for Primitive Methodist Chapel, now situated in the balcony of Christ Church.

50. J. and C. A. Wheeler, Swanland: Recollections of Village Life. 1984, p45.

51. Trustee Minutes Books of Swanland Primitive Methodist Chapel,1898-1966, Hull City Archives, DCT 766.

52. Joint meeting with Great Thornton Street, Hull Methodist Circuit, 1937 to report on closures and mergers, Hull City Archives, DCT 543.

53. Mrs E. Dyson, 1968. A description of village life in Swanland in the early part of the 20th century.

54. Mrs Dyson, op. cit. p60.

55. Mrs Dyson, op.cit. p62.

56. Statistical Survey for Hull and District for Wesleyan Methodism. Hull City Archives, DCT 778, 1887.

57. Foundation stone, now situated at bottom of steps leading to the new vicarage.

58. Reverend Richard Hill in discussion.

59. North Ferriby Church Council minutes and meetings of qualified electors, 1917-1950, East Riding Archives Office, Beverley.

60. Service Book for Swanland Mission Hall/St. Barnabas Church, 1917-1977. East Riding Archives Office, Beverley. PE SO 3/1,2,3,4.

61. North Ferriby and Swanland Parish Magazine, August 1972.

62. Richard Hill, The Story of St. Barnabas New Church Building, leaflet.

APPENDICES

APPENDIX 1

A TRANSCRIPT OF THE COURT ROLLS OF THE MANOR OF SWANLAND FOR THE YEAR 1511 - 1512

The court of **Brian Stapilton & Robert Haldynbe Esquires held there on Tuesday 20th day of the month of April in the third year of the reign of king henry[,]the eighth after the conquest of England[,]in the presence of Robert Constable[,]knight[,]then steward in that place.**

Sworn

Peter Carlett	Richard Aschelot[1]	Laurence Ewbank
Richard Riplynggham	Richard Logan	Robert Logan
Robert Brekilbank	Robert Kerkman	Robert Notbrowne

(Thomas Bakhowsse)	John Mellnar
Robert Hardy	Hugo Johnson
John Wilson	

The Bailiff of the lord is ordered that he should distrain the lands & holding of Walter Rudstun [deceased] in perpetuity & the heir shall come to answer to the lord as to the profit he shall give and to do homage and service to the lord[,]as he was summoned to do at various times[,] & truly settle his land and holding.

Ellerton similarly

Fine 12d In this court they presented that Margaret Paipe has received a quarter part of a wine measure of barley [and] is stealing [it]out of the household of John Robson [and is] therefore in mercy – 12d

Fine 10s The Jurors say that the Prior of Ferebe had four hundred sheep kept under the pastures called the Waldyngges & the pastures called Waldkar & the Ferebye Wald against the ordinance & resolution of an earlier court and is therefore in mercy – 10s

Fine 3s 8d The Jurors say that the Prior [12d] of Ferebe[,] John [12d] Ros Esquire[,] William [8d] Gudknape[,]Alexander [8d] Lound[,]John [2d] Robson & Thomas [2d] Wren[,] each of them[,] owes suit to this court in respect of their lands and has made default [and is] therefore in mercy as [shown] above his name.

{ (The Jurors say,)together with all the men of this lordship[,]that no-one may keep oxen nor sheep under the sown field but on their own lands[,] under appropriate penalty on each and every occasion – 4d

{ It is pained that each person should make six cartings[,] before the feast of St John the Baptist next to come[,]for the making up of the common way under penalty of whosoever [shall default]12d / And [those] who stay in the cottages should collect stones[,]each of them to the making of six cartings[,]under penalty of whichever carting [in default]– 4d. / And that no-one shall keep oxen or trespass with his sheep under the pastures of Ferebe[,]under appropriate penalty on each and every occasion 12d and[,]however[,]of an old woman 4d.

{ And that no-one shall cut down a crop which is anything of the lord's, nor carry [it] away to the boundary hedge of the lord under penalty on each and every occasion 12d
It is pained that no-one may collect ears of grain[, as] of experience in times past he was encouraged [to do,]nor may he collect peas but upon his own land under penalty on each and every occasion 12d

Transcriber's Note: Henry VIII acceded to the throne on 22 April 1509. The third year of his reign therefore began on 22 April 1511, which, strictly speaking, would make the year of this April Court Roll 1512. However, the October Court Roll was clearly written after the April one, and that too is described as being in third year of the reign. It seems likely, therefore, that both records refer to the year 1511 and that the clerk has simply anticipated the start of the new regnal year by two days.

[1] The upper part of this name, as of the others on this row, is obscured by a crease in the document. However, the names can mostly be inferred by comparison of this partial rendering with the jury list for the next sitting of the court recorded below.

The court of Brian Stapilton & Robert Haldynbe Esquires held there on Wednesday 7th day of the month of October in the third year of the reign of king henry[,] the eighth after the conquest of England[,] in the presence of Robert Constable[,] knight[,] then steward in that place.

Sworn

Peter Carlett	Richard Aschelot	John Smythe
Richard Riplynggham	Robert Logan	Robert Hardy
Robert Brekilbank	Richard Logan	Laurence Ewbank

Robert Kerkman
John Wilson
Thomas Bakhowsse

Fines 4s

The jurors bound by oath upon the Holy Gospels say [that] the aforesaid Prior 12d of Ferriby[.] John Ros 12d Esquire[,] Walter 6d Frost Esquire[,] Ellerton 6d & William 6d Gudknape owe suit to this court in respect of their lands under such lordship & whoever does default is therefore in mercy as shown above [his] name. From Alex Lound in respect of [his] oversight – 6d

Fines 9s 8d

And they presented (that)the Prior of Ferriby had two hundred sheep kept under the sown field through his bondsman[,] against the ordinance as appears in earlier courts and to the serious detriment of his neighbours and is therefore in mercy – 4s / Likewise from Peter Carlett in respect of one hundred of his sheep kept under the sown field – 2s / Likewise from Robert Carlyngge in respect of eighty sheep as kept above – 16d / Likewise from Robert Seman in respect of one huncred and twenty sheep held under the agreement – 2s 4d

Fines 9s 4d

And the jurors presented that the Prior of Fereby had sixteen horses kept under the sown field against the ancient resolution & against the consensus of neighbours & to their detriment [and is] therefore in mercy – 5s 4d

Likewise from the said Prior because his servant kept two hundred sheep under the pasture called the Waldyngges to the serious detriment of his neighbours [and is] therefore in mercy – 4s

Fines 20s

The jurors presented that Nicholas Bakhowsse made an attack and an affray upon Richard Wilson and drew blood upon him against the peace of our lord the king [and is] therefore in mercy in respect of the affray 3s 4d and in respect of the drawing of blood 6s 8d.

For the same[,]and from the said Richard Wilson[,] in respect of making an affray upon the said Nicholas[,]in mercy 3s 4d & in respect of the drawing of blood [,] in mercy 6s 8d.

APPENDIX 2

ARCHAEOLOGICAL EXCAVATIONS - MAIN STREET

In July and August 1989 a new building project commenced which included St. Barnabas Church and the houses in St. Barnabas Drive. The field to be used was bounded by Main Street on the south, Beech Hill Road on the east and Beech Hill House on the north. The terrain of this field at the southern end was very rough in nature with a rather steep incline running north to south. The undulating nature had for many years been noted but no one, even practising archaeologists, had given an explanation. It was when the builders *Horncastle Homes* made it known that they were about to build, that Patrick Norfolk approached the writer saying that he had noticed 'house platforms' in the field. The builders told us that a road was to be driven through in two weeks time. They offered us the chance to investigate, which we gratefully accepted. As there was so little time it was decided to excavate as much as possible and draw the plans of whatever was found.

We immediately found a wall footing. This wall was followed round revealing the plan form of a long house. Trenches were dug within the walls but no floor surfaces were found. We noticed several more house platforms and their positions were noted. A plan, Fig. 2, shows where each house was located.

Site 1.
This was the last to be excavated so, slightly more time was spent on this house. Even so many questions remained unanswered.

At the time the south wall was not found as it was hidden by a hedge. Following the excavation a service trench has revealed a wall on the hedge's south side. The north wall had in large part disappeared. The part that remained of the east wall was quite substantial and it was four or five courses high in places. Below the floor level inside this wall was a large area of carbon that contained shards of pottery. The west wall was a single course with a depression in its centre suggesting an entrance. There was a small amount of paved floor in the northern end of the house. It was pleasing to find a hearth on the floor at this point. The brick hearth was surrounded by baked clay and a few stones on the east side of the hearth suggested a slim wall. Outside this building on the north side was a very tumbled down outbuilding. Apart from the area close to the hearth, actual floor levels were difficult to find or non-existent. Because of limited time the floors in the south end of the house were never found nor were the floors in the outbuilding. On the east side of this property ran a high bank and even further east ran the road that linked the back road to the main road.

Site 2.

As opposed to site one, which ran north to south, this property ran east to west. With the exception of the north wall, the rest of the walls of this building were very meagre. No entrances could be found. Outside the east end, another wall ran north south. Once again, due to lack of time and assistance, the rest of the building was not excavated. No floors were found but in the south west corner foundations of an earlier building were observed. This continued under Site 3 and had in fact been cut through to accommodate the later walls.

Site 3.

Like site 2. The south wall was rather poor but it did contain an entrance. On the outside of this entrance was an area of cobbling approx. 3x2 metres. The east wall at its centre almost touched the corner of the west wall in site 2. A jeton (a counter used with an abacus) was found on a floor layer between these buildings. The north wall in places was very substantial. It also had a doorway in its centre. Outside this doorway was a hollow in the steep banking of the backroad. The backroad here runs east to west. Outside of the west wall approximately 2 metres away another substantial wall runs north south. We may never know what this building was like as it now lies under a heavy over burden placed there by the builders.

Between the latter wall and the west wall of site 3 were two ancient surfaces one above the other. On the uppermost, a large quantity of coal had been deposited. Both these levels contained a considerable amount of pottery shards, jn fact much more than was recovered from the rest of the excavation. Most of this can be dated to late 15th early 16th C. the exception being several pieces from 12-13th. C. These could possibly be associated with the earlier building.

Commencing from the paved area on the south side of site 3 was a large area covered with stone rubble perhaps some 30 metres square. A long narrow trench and other exploratory squares were dug to confirm this. Further to the south and running up to the road was a large hollow. This must have been the pond shown on the 1824 enclosure plan. Suggested uses for this metalled area could be a stack yard or a stockade.

Walls were built from both chalk and oolitic limestone, also squared off flints and erratics. The inside area of Site 1 had limestone slabs and chalk around the hearth. Outside the entrance to Site 3, it would appear that the area down the slope to the pond was cobbled.

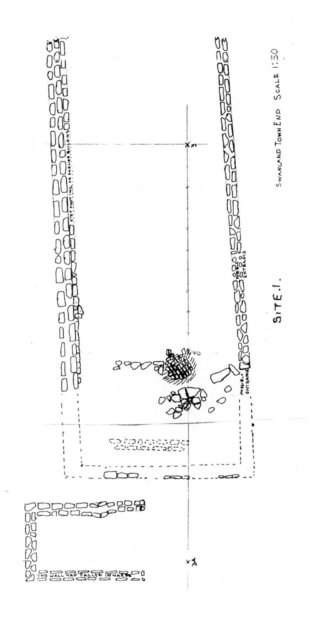

Fig. 38 Site1

111

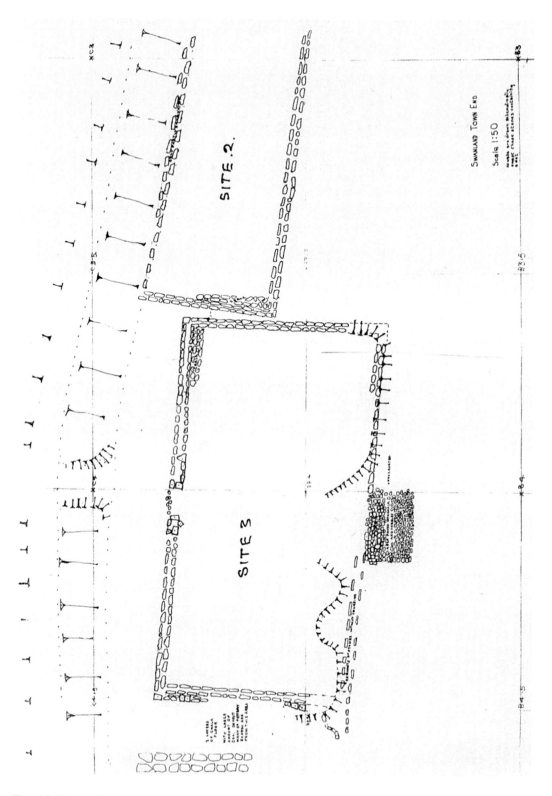

Fig. 39 Sites 2 & 3

112

APPENDIX 3

A BRIEF INTRODUCTION TO MEDIEVAL LAY SUBSIDIES

The word "subsidy" has a nice benevolent ring about it. The Oxford Dictionary defines it as "a sum of money granted to support an undertaking held to be in the public interest". As far as the Lay Subsidies in the late thirteenth and early fourteenth centuries were concerned however, the 'undertaking' that was held to be in the public interest was none other than the Crown. Indeed, one of the alternative dictionary definitions of a subsidy is a "parliamentary grant to the sovereign for state needs". In other words the lay subsidy was, in practice, *a tax*.

Before the thirteenth century, taxes payable by ordinary people were virtually unknown in this country. Of course, the Lord of the manor would demand his rent and manor court fines and the church would demand its tithes; but central government, in the shape of the crown, rarely asked for the type of contribution which corresponded to the present day demands of the Inland Revenue.

It was really Edward I who changed all that. In the closing years of the thirteenth century he became embroiled in costly military campaigns against France and Scotland and the financial demands were so massive that there was no possibility of their being met from the usual sources of Revenue available to the Crown. Edward therefore decided to follow a precedent set very early in the thirteenth century, during the reign of King John, when there had been an occasional tax on personal property or, as it was termed at the time, movable goods. Henry III had repeated the process four times, between 1225 and 1269, and Edward himself had already invoked it twice in 1275 and 1283.[1] The tax demanded from every man in the country, apart from peasants in the most abject poverty, was a sixth, a tenth, or some other fraction of the assessed value of his movable goods. Houses and land, being immovable, were exempt, as also were domestic goods and chattels. However, livestock, grain and other goods, that were potentially saleable and movable from place to place, were all regarded as reckonable and were included in the assessment of liability for tax.

To say that the tax was payable by every 'man' in the country is to use that word advisedly. At that time, married women were not regarded as possessing property in their own right, and the inclusion of single women and self-sufficient widows in the liability for this tax was comparatively rare. Clergy were also exempt, at least as far as their possessions relating to the discharge of their clerical functions were concerned, and hence the designation of the tax as a *Lay* Subsidy.

Collection was the responsibility of two or more officers appointed for each county, the principal taxers or collectors, and reporting to them would usually be two sub-taxers appointed from each local community to carry out the detailed assessments of the inhabitants.[2]

Maddicott[3] has pointed out that, from the 1290s, this levy on movable goods, which had only been an occasional measure during the previous hundred years, became much more frequent and much more onerous. In a period of forty-one years there were sixteen such levies, almost twice the number collected in the century prior to 1294.[3]

It was not only the frequency but also the rate of taxation, which tended to increase, though there was a good deal of variation. Between 1225 and 1290 the rate had varied between a fortieth (1232) and a fifteenth (1225 and 1275), but after 1294 the shires paid at rates that ranged between a ninth in 1297 and a twenty-fifth in 1309; the average rate from 1307 to 1334 was about an eighteenth. It was also in the 1290s that the proceeds of taxation were placed under the direct control of the Exchequer and different rates for town and country were introduced. One result of more expensive wars was thus to make the levy on movables an accepted part of government's resources.[3]

The subsidy was undoubtedly an unfair tax. Its imposition, not on income but on movable goods, meant that those whose livelihoods came mainly from rents probably escaped lightly. Landlords were assessed only on the produce of their own demesnes, or private lands, as Lords of the Manors; and it is possible that the trend away from the direct exploitation of the demesne and towards its leasing out, a change which was taking place on many estates about this time, may be partly explained by the lord's wish to avoid the now frequent levy on movables. Tenants, on the other hand, who needed to produce both to maintain themselves and to find the money for the rents and dues demanded by their lords, could not avoid the tax.[4]

The extent to which the tax was a damaging burden on the general population has been the subject of considerable debate. There is certainly evidence that the Exchequer took steps to limit such damage, though the taxers did not always follow their instructions implicitly.

Firstly, a person was taxed only on those of his goods which were potentially for sale, and not on those needed for his own domestic use. The tax thus reduced his ability to accumulate resources, but was not meant to drive him to starvation. Yet a tenant paying a money rent for his land is likely to have been more heavily taxed than one who met his dues in kind by rendering labour services, since the former would usually need to generate sufficient saleable produce just to pay the rent.[4]

Secondly, each man's goods were usually assessed at well below their market price, often being undervalued by as much as 50 per cent. Since the local sub-taxers were drawn from the villagers, they were probably at pains to minimize the displeasure of their neighbours by making valuations of their goods that were clearly on the low side. There appears to have been general recognition by the authorities that the imposition of a tenth or a fifteenth might yield only a twentieth or a thirtieth of the real market price of the goods assessed.[5]

Thirdly, the Exchequer itself offered some protection for the poorest. After 1294 there was for each subsidy (apart from that taken in 1301) a minimum level of wealth, below which the tax was not imposed. This was usually possession of goods to the value of 10 shillings. Possession of marketable goods worth less than this amount guaranteed exemption from the subsidy. The fact that in some districts the lowest assessment was actually larger than the official minimum suggests that the village sub-taxers sometimes drew the line above that decreed by the Exchequer.[5]

Nevertheless, such considerations do not tell the whole story. The conduct of crown officials, including that of the chief taxers for the counties and the sub-taxers for the villages, was monitored by periodic enquiries; and these enquiries produced considerable evidence of abuse of office. Though there was undoubtedly much under-assessment, on many manors much also disappeared into the pockets of the sub-taxers and was never recorded on any assessment list. For example, the enquiries of 1323-4 disclosed that the sub-taxers of Pickering levied 24s 5d more than they paid to the king; while at Howden the very large sum of 58s was taken and concealed. The emergence of many more such cases throughout the period suggests that the assessment figures do not necessarily give an accurate indication of the weight of the subsidy.[6]

Moreover, the Exchequer's orders for the exemption of the poor did not always afford the intended protection, though sub-taxers sometimes seem to have set a higher level for exemption than that laid down by the government. They may have been taking a more realistic view of their neighbours' ability to pay what was demanded. Just as often, however, they seem to have taxed those whom even the Exchequer would have exempted. In the Lincolnshire enquiry of 1298 the taxation of "non-taxables" is revealed as the commonest malpractice by the sub-taxers, which levied charges as small as 2d on some individuals.[7]

Other misdemeanours on the part of the village sub-taxers were common place. They often saw their temporary office as an opportunity for personal gain. Goods could be assessed at a higher value than that shown on the official record and the difference quietly pocketed. Even so, they might in turn be pressed for unauthorized payments by the chief taxers and collectors, who might not be disposed to accept their accounts unless a shilling or two had been put their way.[8]

Inevitably, such malpractice by the officials meant a heavier burden for the rest of the community. However, it was probably less burdensome, though more generally encountered, than the penalties for non-payment of taxation. In times of financial stringency the crown was particularly forceful in collecting the debts owing to it, including debts for unpaid taxes.[8]

References for Appendix 3

1 J.F.Willard,   *Parliamentary Taxes on Personal Property 1290 to 1394,*
                  Medieval Academy of America, Cambridge, Mass. 1394, p3
2. *Ibid.* pp 33-53
3. J.R.Maddicott, *Past and Present – Supplement 1: The English Peasantry and   the Demands of the*
                  Crown,1294 to 1341, The Past and Present Society, Oxford 1975, p6
4. *Ibid p7*
5. *Ibid p8*
6. *Ibid p9*
7. *Ibid p10*
8. *Ibid p11*

APPENDIX 4

Translation of the will of Elizabeth wife of Thomas de Swanland of Beverley

In the name of God Amen. I Elizabeth wife of Thomas de Swanland of Beverley draper on the Thursday next before the feast of Easter in the year of Our Lord the one thousand four hundred and fourth sound in my mind establish and make my will in this manner.

Firstly I bequeath my soul to Almighty God to the Blessed Virgin Mary and to all the saints of the court of heaven and my body to be buried in the Chapel of the Blessed Mary in Beverley beneath the tombstone of John de Garton formerly my husband.

Also I bequeath to my Vicar 2s. Also I bequeath to the chaplain of the parish 12d. Also I bequeath for the fabric of the said Chapel 3s 4d. Also I bequeath to the minor brothers of Beverley one quarter of malt. Also I bequeath to the aforesaid brothers 3s 4d. Also I bequeath to the poor in the Maisondieu[1] next to the Crossbridge 12d. Also I bequeath to the lepers in the Spittle House[2] outside the North Bar 12d. Also I bequeath to the poor staying in the house of St Giles 6d.

Also I bequeath to Phillip my son one silver belt formerly his father's. Also I bequeath to Annis my daughter one pair of [?] ... with two rings formerly Alice Wryth's. Also I bequeath to Ellen my daughter one gown of dark red with grey fur and one kirtle of the same colour with one hood of scarlet. Also I bequeath to Joanna my daughter one silver belt with a black coating and to the same Joanna one set of beads of silver and coral one white casket and the two best sheets of all my sheets and to the same Joanna two gold rings and one gown of blue trimmed with satin one large chest formerly my mother's. Also I bequeath to the said Joanna my daughter one red tunic lined with violet. Also I bequeath to the same Joanna 100s sterling. Also I bequeath to John my son 100s. Also I bequeath to William my son 100s. Also I bequeath to Alice Roose one plain round ring. Also I bequeath to Annis Yhole half a piece of henna velvet and one pair of small knives ornamented with silver. Also I bequeath to Agnes of John Marshall one green tunic and one hood of dark red. Also I bequeath to Joanna my servant one russet gown trimmed with much fur. Also I bequeath to Ellen my maid one green gown with a hood. Also I bequeath to Margaret Wade one [?] of pleated velvet. Also I bequeath to

---

[1] Maisondieu (*French: 'God's house'*) mentioned in various sources and thought to be St Mary's Hospital.
[2] Believed to have stood on the land now occupied by 15 to 21 North Bar Without.

William my apprentice 3s 4d. Also I bequeath to Alice formerly my seamstress one [?] of velvet one hood of blue. Also I bequeath to Alice of Walkington half [?] a piece of dressed [candlewick??] one long blanket.

Also I bequeath to Robert de Swanland one gold ring. And for well and faithfully giving effect to such my will in full measure I appoint and make Thomas de Swanland my husband my sole executor that he himself may arrange [matters] for [the good of] my soul according as he can best deliver before God. These being witnesses Thomas Roos and William Ellis. Given at Beverley on the day and in the year abovesaid.

The present will was proved [on the] second day of the month of April in the year of Our Lord abovesaid and committed to the executor named in the same will in form of law.

York Probate Records (913), Volume 3, Folio 105

APPENDIX 5
Translation of the will of John Coke late of Swanland deceased

In the name of God Amen. The twelfth day of the month of January in the year of Our Lord the one thousand five hundred [and] seventh.

I John Coke of Swanland [being] sound of mind but now reflecting on the fragility of mankind [and] considering that nothing [is] more certain than death[,]intercepted at the hour of death[,] I make my will in this manner. Firstly I bequeath and indeed commit my soul to Almighty God to the Blessed Virgin Mary and to all the saints of the court of heaven [,] the body that is mine to be buried in the southern part of the church of the community of all saints of North Ferriby next to the rowans with my best beast in the name of my mortuary. Also I bequeath in respect of one canopy over against the sacrament spread above that which is to be served upon the alter 3s 4d and for the fabric of my parish church 3s 4d. Also I bequeath to the chapel of the Blessed Mary of Swanland 3s 4d.

Also I bequeath to the boy to whom I am godfather[,] annually from baptism until he is confirmed before the face of the church 4d. Also I bequeath to Johanna Newsome my maid two quarters of barley. However the remainder of all my goods not bequeathed in this will for my specified obligations I give and bequeath to Agnes my wife for setting in order for the good of my soul whom I make and confirm [to be] my executrix that my trust may work in her. Given at Swanland on the day and in the year abovesaid, these being witnesses: John Sherwood William Kirkman John Smith of Swanland and others.

In the name of God Amen. Admitted to probate before our Dean of Harthill and Hull. We pronounce and declare proved and we truly declare the administration of all goods of the selfsame deceased lying within our jurisdiction and the authority of our commission.................. [to be] committed to the executrix named in the same will after the manner of the disposal of legacies in this case. In which testamentary matter our seal of office is affixed to these presents. Given at North Ferriby the twenty-third day of the month of February in the year of Our Lord the one thousand five hundred and seventh.

York Probate Records (Microfilm 917) Volume 7 Folio 23

APPENDIX 6

Administration of the estate of Isabel Haldenby

Commital in [respect of] the goods of Isabel Haldenby late of Swanland deceased

Likewise on the seventh day of the month of December in the year of Our Lord the one thousand four hundred and fifty-third was committed the administration of all the goods of Isabel Haldenby late of Swanland[,] in view of the intestacy of the deceased[,] to Robert Haldenby and Thomas Haldenby sons and administrators in the goods of the same deceased. Noted to have been considered by the Ordinary and judged in form of law etc.

York Probate Records Volume 2 Folio 2871

APPENDIX 7

Translation of the will of Nicholas Kirkman lately of Swanland deceased

In the name of God Amen and being about to enter upon the hosts of the Catholic faith which undoubtedly I acknowledge and always firmly believe and all the articles of the same I hold and indeed .... with soundness of mind thinking myself right to hold[,] and in all [things] to believe[, which] they say Holy mother church believes and teaches must be believed ...... with faith.

I Nicholas Kirkman of Swanland [being] of sound mind [on this] twentieth day of the month of December in the year of Our Lord the one thousand four hundred and fifty-eighth do make my will in this manner following. Firstly I bequeath my soul to almighty God the blessed Mary and all the Saints and my body to be buried in the parish church of All Saints North Ferriby and in the name of my mortuary attached to my goods. Also I bequeath to the lord of North Ferriby for tithes foolishly forgotten half an acre of fine wheat. Also I bequeath to the prior 12d. Also I bequeath to the presbyter, in his personal capacity, ministering in the same place, 6d. Also to the parish clerk 4d. Also to the boy, in his personal capacity, 2d. Also I bequeath wine to the Chaplain for celebrating [masses] in the parish church of North Ferriby[,] during one year when it is able to be done fittingly[,] 7 enjoined. Also I give & bequeath to the church of Saint Peter 12d. I bequeath for the fabric of the parish church of North Ferriby one quarter of malt. Also I bequeath to the chapel of Swanland 12d. Also to our vicars 12d.

Also I give and bequeath to Richard my son 20s together with a heifer. Also I bequeath to Emmott wife of the said Richard 4 breeding ewes. Also I bequeath to Robert my son 20s[,]to his wife 4 breeding ewes. Also I bequeath to John my son 20s together with a heifer. Also I bequeath to Thomas my son 14s 4d together with a heifer. Also I bequeath to Joanna my elder daughter one cow and to each of her [own] children one ewe. Also I bequeath to Joanna my younger daughter one quarter of barley. However the remainder of all my goods in this will not [already] bequeathed [is] at the disposal of Annette my wife and John Peryn whom I ordain and appoint my executors that they .... may have and distribute it for the good of my soul and as may seem to them best in charitable works. Given at Swanland on the day and in the year above stated these being witnesses Robert ..... and Simon Sherwood and others.

The will was proved in person on the third day of the month of January in the year of Our Lord above stated and the administration committed to Annette the widow of the selfsame deceased[,]named as executrix in the same will[,] sworn in form of law by John Perin the other [person] named in the office of coexecutor in the will ....
York Wills Volume 2 Folio 389

APPENDIX 8

Translation of the will of Richard Kirkman lately of Swanland deceased

In the name of God Amen. On the first day of June in the year of our Lordthe one thousand four hundred [and] eighty first.[i] I Richard Kirkman of Swanland husbandman [being] fearful [in] body and sound [in] memory make my will in this manner.

First of all I give and bequeath my soul to the Almighty[,] the Blessed Virgin Mary and all their saints[ii] and my body to be buried in the northern part of the parish church of North Ferriby by the crucifix in that place. Also I bequeath [in] the name of my mortuary my best beast. Also I wish that three pounds of wax may be burnt[iii] beside my body [on] the day of my burial and on the seventh day. Also I bequeath to the Prior[,]the lord of North Ferriby aforesaid[,] for my forgotten tithes and for whatever other offences as may be done against the aforesaid lord[,] one acre of fine wheat lying in the field of Swanland aforesaid next to one acre of Robert Darling of Swanland above stated lying at Hesslewood and beside the Humber.[iv] Also I bequeath for the fabric of the parish church of North Ferriby aforesaid one quarter of malt. Also I bequeath to the chapel of the Blessed Mary at Swanland[v] aforesaid half a quarter of malt. However[,] the remainder of all my goods not [previously] bequeathed I give and bequeath to Emmott my wife and to Robert my brother whom I ordain and appoint my executors that they may faithfully order [matters] for the good of my soul and of all my benefactions according as they shall see fit to deliver.[vi] These being witnesses[:] Master John Baynton Vicar of North Ferriby aforesaid[,] Master John Atkinson chaplain[,] Robert Kirkman[,] John Smyth and others of Swanland aforesaid. Given at Swanland aforesaid on the day of the month and in the year of Our Lord above stated.

The will proved in person [this] fourteenth day of the month of July in the year of Our Lord above stated and the administration committed to the executors named [and] commissioned in the same will in the form of law [sworn … etc][vii]

i Latin wills usually specify the year in the ordinal form.

ii In the late fifteenth century England was still a Catholic country. In post-reformation wills the soul of the testator is more usually dedicated "to Almighty God, my Creator and Redeemer".

iii This was the usual wording of a request for candles to be lit.

iv This location, on the Humber bank, was in the far south-eastern part of the manor of Swanland.

v This appears to be the only reference yet known to the dedication of Swanland's chapel.

vi Literally: "according as it shall be seen by them fit to deliver".

vii Abbreviation of the legal wording with which probate statements usually end.

York Wills Volume 5 Folio 109 – Microfilm 91

APPENDIX 9
Translation of the will of Sir Gerard Usflete knight

In the name of god Amen on the fifteenth day of September in the year of Our Lord the one thousandth four hundredth and fifth. I Gerard de Ousefleet knight being in possession of my mind [and] in good health of body make and ordain my testament in this manner. Firstly I bequeath my soul to God to the Blessed Mary and to all the saints my body however to be buried in of the convent church of North Ferriby and that 4s is for my mortuary. Also I bequeath to the church of York 20s. Also I bequeath for the fabric of the church of Ferriby 20s. Also I bequeath for the fabric of the church of Adlingfleet 20s. Also I bequeath for the fabric of the church of Whitgift 20s. Also I bequeath to the 4 orders of mendicant brothers at Beverley and [?] 4 pounds. Also I bequeath to the Prior of Ferriby 20s. Also I bequeath to the vicar of the same place 6s 8d and to [him] who [is] precentor of the same house 6s 8d. Also I bequeath to the clerk of Ferriby 2s and to the clerk of the Abbey 3s. Also I bequeath for one chaplain for celebrations for my soul for six years in the convent church of North Ferriby and at the altar in the northern part of the church 34 pounds being received in annual payments from my executors. Also I bequeath to Margaret Curtis 5 pounds. Also I bequeath for distribution to the poor £6 13s 4d. Also I bequeath for my funeral offices 10s and on the day of my burial for my neighbours bound to honour my body 10 pounds. Also I bequeath one acre of land at the eastern end of the vill of Swanland for the support of a light before Our Lady in the chapel of Swanland in perpetuity. Also I bequeath for the fabric of the collegiate church of Beverley 20s. Also I bequeath to the chaplain of the parish of Ferriby 3s 4d. Also I bequeath to Anne my daughter 100 marks. Also I bequeath to Isabella my daughter 100 marks. Also I bequeath to Leonard my son 10 pounds and to John my son £6 13s 4d. Also I bequeath to Aniana mother of the same John if so it be that she stay with me until the day of my burial 5 pounds otherwise not. Also I bequeath to my servants 5 pounds each at the arrangement and direction of my executors. Also I bequeath to the hospital of Saint Thomas ...... in .... 20s. Also I bequeath to Gerard my son my best bed with .....one with my best covering and one silver gilt cup with the tall base and with the lid of the same with the large .... Also I bequeath to Ann my daughter one silver gilt cup with the lid of the same in .... Also I bequeath to Isabella my daughter one silver gilt cup with the lid of the same and if it happens that Gerard my son ..... should have wished anything else from my goods I will that .... he may have for eighteen shillings that which others ought to give 20s. Also I bequeath to my executors 10 pounds for the management of my testamentary affairs. This will I wish to be fulfilled by the discovering of my goods however before they be divided by the executors if goods were not [avail]able to fulfil [it]. The remainder of my goods not bequeathed I bequeath and settle according to the arrangement of my executors namely of Thomas Egmanton[,] Sir John Vicar of Sancton[,] Sir William Havelot[,]William Freboye[,]William Gunsyn[,] John my Bailiff and Peter the cotter on condition that they order and assemble my remaining goods[,] bequeathed and unbequeathed that should have been[,] according as [seems] best to them namely for the good of my soul and the lives of all my beneficiaries and of all the faithful deceased I appoint as overseers beforehand of this will Sir John of Ousefleet[,] Reo...... of Beckingham & Gerard my son that they may see that the fully aforesaid my executors may fulfil my will towards the sum of my goods through full agreement as aforesaid. In witness of which[,] properly of my [own] wish[,] to this public testament I have affixed my seal by my own hand. Given at Swanland [on] the day and [in] the year of Our Lord abovesaid.

Proved was this will on the 5th day of the month of April in the year of Our Lord one thousand four hundred and six and committed to William Freeboye[,] Sir John Vicar of Sancton and Peter the Cotter[,] executors sworn in form of law.

York Probate Records

APPENDIX 10

Translation of a writ of *certiorari* (1369) issued by Edward III in respect of a

tenancy dispute concerning Cecilia of Swanland

Edward, by the grace of God King of England, Lord of Ireland and Aquitaine, to his wellbeloved and faithful John Ruynet, his Chief Justice, greeting. Wishing to be informed about the issues determined , and to consider the course of events and the progress of the return of verbal evidence which was before us [in the matter] between us and Cecilia, who was the wife of John son of Richard of Swanland, regarding a holding in Swanland seised into our hand by John de Scotherskelf, lately our Escheator in the county of York, we command you to consider the course of events and indeed the progress of the return of evidence aforesaid and all things touching upon these matters in our chancery and you shall send [your judgement] under your distinctive seal without delay with this writ attached. Witnessed by myself at Westminster this 8th day of February in the third and fortieth year of our reign.

National Archives C 260/80(No.6)

APPENDIX 11 Introduction to Heraldry

Any noble family could apply to the College of Heralds for a Coat of Arms or Blazon and had to comply to their rules and was described in a heraldic language. This brief resume gives an outline to this.

Tinctures these are the colours used on blazons. There were two metals plus colours, when carved in stoneware they were depicted symbolically; this was known as trick.

 Metals: Gold (or) trick dots
   Silver (argent abbreviation arg) trick plane
 Colours: Blue (azure abbr. Az) trick horizontal lines
   Red (gules abrv. Gu) trick vertical lines
   Black (sable abrv. sa) trick vertical & horizontal lines
   Green (vert abrv.vert) trick diagonal lines top left to bottom right
   Purple (purpure abrv. purp.) trick diagonal lines top right to bottom left
Occasionally two other staines:
   Orange (Tenny) trick vertical and diagonal top right to bottom left
   Murray (Sanguine Red Blood) trick diagonal lines both way
 There were also furs depicted as:
  Ermine Black spots on white
  Erminous Black spots on Gold
  Pean Gold Spots on Black
  Vair Blue and white alternate castelations
  Countervair same with mirrored image on next line
  Potent like a letter T
  Counterpotent an inverted letter T

Rules of Blazon are, the field of the shield should be first described the colour of the field the main charge then subsidiary charges chief and charges on the chief. Metals are never on colours.

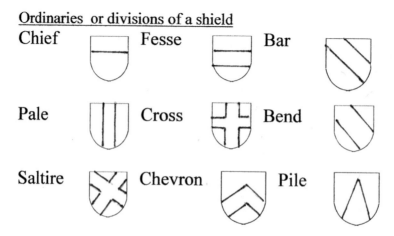

Ordinaries or divisions of a shield

Chief   Fesse   Bar

Pale   Cross   Bend

Saltire   Chevron   Pile

APPENDIX 12

MINISTERS WHO HAVE SERVED CHRIST CHURCH

Taken from the pamphlet 'Christ Church, Swanland' written by Raymond Taylor and John White

1696 – 1702	Rev. Emanuel Dewsnop
1703 -	Rev. Brook
- 1713	Rev. Gardner
1715 – 1728?	Rev. Joshua Hardcastle
1720 – 1738	Rev. Joshua Hoyle
1740 - ?	Rev. John Angiers. Died 1780 at Swanland
1770 – 1773	Rev. Samuel Bottomley
1775 - 1782	Rev. George Gill
1783 – 1785	Rev. Richard Leggett
1786 – 1827	Rev. David Williams
1826 – 1834	Rev. John Haydon
1835 – 1844	Rev. John Evison
1844 – 1850	Rev. John Bramall
1851 – 1853	Rev. Robert Thomson, M.A.
1854 – 1865	Rev. James Wishart, M.A.
1866 – 1866	Rev. E. Newman
1867 – 1871	Rev. George Snashall, B.A.
1872 – 1899	Rev. J. E. Whitehead
1899 – 1914	Rev. Wm. St. John Crickmer
1914 – 1922	Rev. Wm. Nicholson
1922 – 1924	Rev. R. J. Hill
1924 – 1928	Rev. T. Langham Moore
1929 – 1946	Rev. John G. Patton
1946 – 1950	Rev. D. Trevor Roberts
1950 – 1956	Rev. Albert F. Bayly, B.A.
1958 – 1961	Rev. Derek A. Fitch
1961 – 1964	Pastor Rowland V. F. Taylor
1965 – 1971	Rev. W. K. Gathercole, M.A., B.D.

1971 – 1975	Pastor H. K. Johnson
1975 – 1978	Rev. David Anderson, B.A.
1979 – 1981	Rev. Harry Smith, U.R.C. Interim Moderator
	Rev. Derek Jennings, Methodist Minister
1981 – 1988	Rev. Kenneth Marshall
1988 – 1991	Rev. Stanley Barker, B.A.
1991 – 1994	Rev. Kingsley Halden, M.A
1994 – 1996	Rev. Philip Chilvers
1996 – 1998	Rev. Steven Knapton, M.A. Interim Moderator
1998 – 2001	Rev. Ian Jones, B.Sc., B.Th.
2002 – 2004	Rev. Sue M. Sowden, B. Min. Th.
2004 - 2005	Rev. Shirlyn Toppin
2005 -	Rev. Denise Free

APPENDIX 13

Sources of found references to De SWANLAND in chronological order

Source:	Abbreviation:
CATALOGUE OF ANCIENT DEEDS	AD
ASSIZE ROLLS	AR
BRITISH ARCHIVES	BA
BORTHWICK INSTITUTE (YORK UNIVERSITY)	BI
COMMONERS' ARMS in ENGLAND	CAE
CORPORATION of LONDON RECORDS OFFICE	CLRO
CALENDAR of CLOSE ROLLS	CR
DRAPERS' COMPANY	DCo
FINES	F
HULL ARCHIVES	HA
HULL UNIVERSITY ARCHIVES	HUA
INQUISITIONS	I
LAY SUBSIDY ROLLS	LS
CALENDAR of PATENT ROLLS	PR
VICTORIAN COUNTY HISTORY OF HERTFODSHIRE	VCH-H
WESTMINSTER ABBEY MUNIMENTS	WAM

EDWARD I (1272-1307)

1282	Simon de Swanelonde	
14 Feb 1288	Grant to Simon de Swanneslund - doc witnessed by Richard Bradan	WAM
1 Aug 1298	John de Swanland - became vicar in Thoresweye	WAM
1 Apr 1300	John de Swanlunde	PR
9 Feb 1302	Thomas, son of Geoffrey of Swanlond - granted king's pardon for murder	PR
9 Feb 1302	Pardon given to Gervaise, son of Alice de Mercato, for death of Thomas, son of Geoffrey of Swanlond	PR

EDWARD II (1307-1327)

16 Jul 1309	Simon de Swanelund	WAM
8 Mar 1311	Simon de Swanlund, Citizen and Merchant of London	WAM
6 Jul 1311	Stephen, son of John of Swanland	PR
12 Nov 1314	John de Swanneslund- resigned as vicar	PR
20 Nov 1314	Simon de Swanlond	CR
16 Apr 1315	John de Swanlund, clerk - claiming ancient land rights	PR
20 Apr 1315	Simon de Swanlond - merchant selling cloth to king (£171 13s 4d)	CR
24 Apr 1315	Simon de Swanlond - owed and paid £2000; also £400	CR
25 Apr 1315	Simon de Swanlond - owed 100 marks	CR

20 May 1315	Simon de Swanlond - owes £2000	CR
3 Jun 1315	Simon de Swanelond - act as attorney	PR
28 July 1315	Nicholas, son of John of Swanneslound also Stephen his brother broke dykes at Myton	PR
29 Sept 1315	Simon de Swanlund	WAM
24 Oct 1315	Simon de Swanlund, Citizen and Merchant of London	WAM
28 Oct 1315	Simon de Swanlund, Citizen and Merchant of London	WAM
2 Nov 1315	Simon de Swanlond - demand for 2000 marks to be paid by King of France after piracy	CR
11 Nov 1315	Simon de Swanlund, Citizen and Merchant of London	WAM
11 Nov 1315	Simon de Swanlund, Citizen and Burgess of London	WAM
16 Nov 1315	Simon de Swanlund, Citizen and Burgess of London	WAM
30 Nov 1315	Simon de Swanlund, Citizen and Merchant of London	WAM
3 Feb 1316	Simon de Swanlund - nominated as attorney	PR
20 Feb 1316	Nicholas, son of John of Swanneslound also Stephen his brother broke dykes at Myton	PR
22 Mar 1316	Simon de Swanlond - owed £50	CR
25 Mar 1316	Simon de Swanlound, Citizen and Merchant of London	WAM
25 Apr 1316	Simon de Swanlound	WAM
14 Jun 1316	Simon de Swanlund - owed £2000	CR
20 July 1316	Simon de Swanlond, king's yeoman	PR
10 Oct 1316	John de Swanlund, clerk, Simon de Swanlund and Nicholas de Swanlund	PR
10 Oct 1316	Loretta, late wife of John de Usfleet, Nicholas, son of John de Swanneslond and Stephen, his brother .....broke dykes at Myton	PR
08 Mar 1317	Simon de Swanlund, Citizen of London	WAM
12 Mar 1317	Simon de Swanlund, Citizen of London	WAM
24 Mar 1317	Simon de Swanlund, Merchant of London	WAM
25 Mar 1317	Simon de Swanlund, Citizen and Merchant of London	WAM
6 May 1317	Simon de Swanland - owed and paid £10	CR
21 May 1317	Simon de Swanlund, Citizen and Merchant of London	WAM
19 Jun 1317	Simon de Swanlund, Merchant of London	WAM
2 Sep 1317	Simon de Swanlaund - referred to as king's merchant. Granted tax relief	CR
28 Sep 1317	Simon de Swanlund	WAM
17 Oct 1317	Simon de Swanlond - owed £40	CR
18 Oct 1317	Simon de Swanlund	WAM
20 Nov 1317	Simon de Swanlund, Citizen and Merchant of London	WAM
1317 - 1318	Simon Swanlond, Citizen and Merchant of London, purchased a part of the manor in North Mimms	VCH-H
8 Feb 1318	Simon de Swanlond - citizen of London, with land in Hertford	CR
26 Feb 1318	Simon de Swanland - citizen of London	CR
13 Apr 1319	Simon de Swanlound - Citizen and Merchant of London	WAM
24 Jun 1319	Simon de Swanlound	WAM

17 Aug 1319	Simon de Swanlound	WAM
30 Nov 1319	Simon de Swanlound - Lord	WAM
1320	Simon de Swanlond - buying and taking wool to Flanders	CR
2 Feb 1320	Simon de Swanlond citizen of London	WAM
20 Feb 1320	Simon de Swanlond - Citizen and Merchant of London	WAM
1 Feb 1321	Simon de Swanlond - owed £701	CR
2 Feb1321	Simon de Swanlond - Citizen and Merchant of London	WAM
7 Jun 1321	Symon de Swanlound - Citizen and Merchant of London	WAM
24 Jun 1321	Simon de Swanlond - Citizen of London	WAM
5 Dec 1321	Simon de Swanlond - had delivered to him 18 and a half pieces of cloth	CR
2 Feb 1322	Simon de Swannelunde - Citizen of London	WAM
12 Mar 1322	Simon de Swanlunde	WAM
25 Mar 1322	Symon de Swanlunde - Citizen of London	WAM
11 Apr 1322	Symon de Swanlunde - Citizen of London (and Richard Bradan)	WAM
15 Apr 1322	Simon de Swannelond - Citizen of London (and Richard Bradan)	WAM
15 Dec 1323	Simon de Swanlond - (with 4 other merchants) suing King of France for 2000 marks	PR
20 Jan 1324	Simon de Swanlond - 1000 marks paid, rest to be paid by Christmas	PR
12 Mar 1324	Simon de Swannelond - Citizen of London	WAM
29 Jun 1324	Richard de Swanneslaunde	WAM
6 Dec 1325	Simon de Swannelond	WAM
6 July ?	John de Swanland + 2 others fined 10s for assault on Richard de Anlaby	PR

EDWARD III (1327-1377)

	In the reign of Edward III (no dates)	
	mention of Loretta de Swanneslaund	I
	mention of John de Swanland and his wife Maud	I
	mention of Cecily, late wife of Nicolas, son of John, and Robert, son of Nicolas	I
	mention of John de Swanland attending a baptism	I
	mention of Simon de Swanlond, knight	I
	mention of William de Swanlond and Isabel, widow of John de Swanlond	I
	mention of Thomas de Swanland and his wife Isabel, daughter of Walter Waldeschef	I
1327	Simon de Swanlond (and Richard Bradan)	WAM
1327-34	Simon de Swanland - draper and alderman of London for Candlewick Ward	CLRO + CAE
12 Mar 1327	Simon de Swanlond - chaplain to celebrate masses for him, his ancestors and heirs paid for in North Mymms	PR
15 April 1327	Simon de Swanlond - ref to him as Lord Mayor of London	PR
14 May 1327	Simon de Swanlonde - quit for life of all taxes from late king and present king	PR
29 Jun 1327	Simon de Swanlonde - quit for life of all taxes from late king and present king	CR
23 July ?	Simon de Swanlond - ref to him as Lord Mayor of London	PR
1 Aug 1327	Symon de Swanlond	WAM
1328	Simon Swanlond founded a chantry in the chapel of St Katherine in the Parish Church of North Mimms Hertfordshire. (pg 260)	VCH-H

11 Aug 1328	Simon de Swanlonde - citizen and merchant of London - owed	
	Thomas de Swanlonde -citizen and merchant of London -and paid John	
	de Swanlonde - parson of Middleton church in the diocese of York £1200 to	
	Nicholas de Swanlonde - John's brother	CR
25 Nov 1328	Simon de Swanlond - Lord of Northmimmes	WAM
1 Dec 1328	Simon de Swanlound - Lord of Northmmmes	
	(Chantry deed ratified by Bishop)	WAM
12 Mar 1329	Simon de Swanlond - Citizen of London	WAM
1329	John de Swanlund, clerk	F
1329	John de Swanland and John Bradan	HUA
1329-1330	Simon de Swanland - Mayor of London	CLRO+ CAE
27 Jan 1330	Thomas de Swanland - ref land in North Mymms	PR
29 Jun 1330	Simon de Swanland - Mayor of London	WAM
2 Jan 1331	Simon de Swanland - citizen of London	CR
28 Jan 1331	John de Swanlond - clerk, owed money from late king for	
	goods bought for his wardrobe	CR
Feb 1331	John de Swanlond - clerk, buying "divers things for the king"	CR
Feb 1331	Simon de Swanlond - late Mayor of London and escheator in the city	CR
8 Mar 1331	John de Swanland - bought land in Huntingdon	CR
13 Mar 1331	Simon de Swanlund - citizen of London, owed £40	CR
15 Mar 1331	Thomas de Swanlund - citizen of London owed £14	CR
27 Mar 1331	Simon de Swanlund - owed £1000 John de Swanland -	
	clerk asked by Alice Lespicer to pursue a debt for her	CR
	Thomas de Swanlond - owed £10	CR
25 Nov 1331	Simon de Swanlond - Lord of Northmymmes	WAM
18 Oct 1332	Simon de Swanlund - Lord of Herefeld -document	
	witnessed by Richard Bradan	WAM
	Simon de Swanlond settled the manor at North Mimms on his	
1332	Children John, William, Simon, Thomas, Maud and Katherine.	VCH-H
25 Mar 1333	Simon de Swanlund, re wood called Woechenham + ref to	
	Richard Bradan	WAM
12 Jun 1333	Thomas de Swanlund - citizen of London, owes £50 to	
	Archbishop of York	CR
10 Feb 1336	Loretta de Swaneslond - mention	CR
1 May 1336	Thomas de Swanlond of London - citizen , owes 100	
	marks from land in London	CR
15 Aug 1336	Simon de Swanlond was witness to document	WAM
29 Sep 1336	Thomas de Swanlund - citizen of London, owns property in	
	County of York	CR
5 Feb 1337	Simon de Swanlond + Richard Bradan were witnesses to document	WAM
3 Mar 1337	Simon de Swanland - knighted	CLRO+CAE
12 Mar 1337	Simon de Swanland - was witness to a document	CR
1337	John de Swanland - clerk of the works of the king's castles and	
1338	towns in Scotland	C
4 Jan 1338	Thomas de Swanlond - citizen of London permitted to take	
	10 sacks of wool to that city	CR
8 Jan 1338	Thomas de Swanlond - citizen and merchant of London - servants	
	given protection tobring wool from ports of Lincoln and London	
	(until Easter)	PR
12 Mar 1338	Thomas de Swanlonde - collector in the port of London	CR
16 Apr 1338	Simon de Swanlonde - pardonned for not having taken the Order of	

	Knighthood by Ascension Day as required by the king's proclamation	PR
1 May 1338	Thomas de Swanlund - collector of customs	CR
8 May 1338	Thomas de Swanlond - collector of the ancient custom in the port of London	C
4 Feb 1339	John de Swanland - king's clerk	CR
17 Apr 1339	Thomas de Swanlond - collector of the ancient custom in the port of London	CR
20 Apr 1339	Simon de Swanlonde - quit for life of all taxes (from 12 July)	CR
14 May 1339	Thomas de Swanlond - collector of the ancient custom in the port of London	CR
4 June 1339	Simon de Swanlond - ref to manor in Northmymmes	CR
25 Jun 1339	Simon de Swanlond - attendant of king, ready to set out with Edward, Duke of Cornwall	CR
11 Aug 1339	Thomas de Swanlond - collector in the port of London, given authority to search, seize and forfeit	PR
13 Aug 1339	Thomas de Swanlond - collector in the port of London	CR
6 Sep 1339	Thomas de Swanlond - collector in the port of London	PR
6 Oct 1339	Thomas de Swanlond - collector in the port of London	CR
7 Oct 1339	Simon de Swanlond - involved in court case	CR
1340+/or1344	Simon de Swanlond - MP for Middlesex	CLRO
28 Feb 1340	Simon de Swanlond - no plea found against him	CR
10 Mar 1340	John de Swanlond - paid by king for importing wool	CR
17 Apr 1340	Thomas de Swanlond- collector in the port of London	CR
10 Aug 1340	Thomas de Swanlond- collector in the port of London	CR
16 Aug 1340	Thomas de Swanlond- collector in the port of London	CR
27 Sep 1340	Thomas de Swanlond- collector in the port of London	CR
26 Jan 1341	Thomas de Swanland - late collector of customs in the port of London	CR
8/5, 1 + 11/9	Thomas de Swanland - late collector of customs in the port of London	CR
15 Jun 1341	John de Swanland the elder - ref to	CR
4 Jun 1342	William de Swanlund - parson of Lutheburgh church has property in County of Lincoln	CR
13 Aug 1342	John de Swanlond and Matilda his wife - a reference to	CR
20 Nov 1342	Thomas de Swanlond - collectors of customs in the port of London	CR
17 Feb 1346	Nicholas de Swanlond of London as a draper	CR
7 Mar 1346	Simon de Swanland has sons - John + William	CR
7 Mar 1346	John de Swanland has wife Maud	CR
8 Oct 1346	Robert, son of Nicholas de Swanlund, weigher Ref to Simon Swanlond owning three parts of the capital manor of North Mimms	VCH-H
18 Jul 1352	(Stannywell) says "Robert, son of Nicholas, son of John of Swanland sold land in Hull"	HA
8 Feb 1355	Rex v Swanland (Cecilia, wife of John, son of Peter of Swanland)	BA
1365	William de Swanlond and his wife Joan owned land in Hull	F
1367	William de Swanlond and his wife Joan	F
1367	William de Swanlond - Lord of Swanlond	WAM

RICHARD 11 (1377-1399)

6 Nov 1377	William Swanlond - became Commissioner of the Peace	PR
15 Nov 1377	Thomas de Swanneslond, merchant (had land seized to pay debt)	PR
6 July 1378	William Swanlond , Commissioner of the Peace in Middlesex	PR
18 Mar 1379	William Swanlond , Commissioner of the Peace in Royston	PR
10 Mar 1380	Thomas de Swanlond, merchant (messuage and landseized to pay debt)	PR

26 May 1380	William Swanlonde, Commissioner of the Peace in Middlesex	PR
1382	William Swanlond , Commissioner of the Peace	PR
1385	William de Swanlond - Lord of Swanlond	WAM
24 Jun 1386	Robert Swanland of Lincoln, king's pardon for murder	PR
27 Jun 1387	Robert de Swaneslonde of Lincoln, king's pardon for murder	PR
10 Feb 1389	William Swanlond, appointed to position in Middlesex	PR
12 May 1390	Nicholas Swanland - late chaplain in St Cuthbert by Layerthorpebrigg	PR
16 May 1390	Robert Swanland - chaplain in Linclon	PR
12 Dec 1390	Robert Swanland - defendant in court case	PR
26 Oct 1391	John Swanlond, surjian of Londdon - non appearance in court over debt	PR
30 May 1392	Robert de Swanlond - defendant in court case	PR
18 Nov 1393	Simon de Swanland, merchant - granted pardon	PR
29 Jan 1394	Simon de Swanland, merchant - grant of free warren	PR
14 Feb 1394	Robert Swanlond of Salisbury - for not appearing re a debt	PR
4 Apr 1396	Nicholas Swanland, chaplain - licensed to found a chantry	PR
1396	Thomas Swannelond of North Mimms, merchant (a mention)	PR
22 Nov 1398	Thomas Swanlond of Bristol, wolmanger - pardon (if ransom paid to King)	PR

HENRY IV (1399-1413)

1402	William Swanland, Manor of Harefield (pg284)	LS
9 Apr 1404	Will of Elizabeth, wife of Thomas de Swanland, draper of Beverley	BI
1404 - 1405	William de Swanlond (son of William) - Lord of Swanlond	WAM
5 July 1408	Thomas Swanland - complaints against him for "flyposting" in Beverley	PR
8 July 1412	Thomas Swanland - complaints against him by Bishop of Durham re Walkington lands	PR

HENRY V (1413-1422)

1418	William de Swanlond - Lord of Swanlond	WAM
13 Jun 1419	William Swanland was lord of the manor of North Mymms	AD
24 Oct 1421	William Swanland esquire, claiming right to land in North Mymms	AD
1421	William de Swanlond - Lord of Swanlond	WAM

HENRY VI (1422-1471)

1422	transfer of land at Mimms	CR
30 April 1429	(Stannywell) land in Munkgate sold to 4 including Thomas Swanland	HA
27 Oct. 1438	(Stannywell) 4 people, including Thomas Swanland, sold land in Marketgate and Munkgate	HA

INDEX